Cross Country Skiing

Sindre Bergan
and Bob O'Connor

MASTERS PRESS

A Division of Howard W. Sams & Company

Published by Masters Press
A Division of Howard W. Sams & Company
2647 Waterfront Pkwy E. Dr, Suite 100, Indianapolis, IN 46214

96 97 98 99 00 01   10 9 8 7 6 5 4 3 2 1

Library of Congress Cataloging-in-Publication Data

Bergan, Sindre.
    Cross country skiing / Sindre Bergan and Bob O'Connor.
        p.   cm.
    ISBN 1-57028-099-1 (trade)
    1. Cross-country skiing. I. O'Connor, Robert II. Title.
    GV885.3.B47   1996   96-51762
    796.93'2--dc21   CIP

Table of Contents

Credits

Edited by Kathleen Prata
Cover Design by Scott Stadler
Text Layout and Design by Kim Heusel

Acknowledgments

We would like to acknowledge: Gehard Pagels who took many of the photographs; Halldor Skard and Olle Larsson who allowed us to use many of their photos; and again to Halldor for allowing our use of his special montage technique for showing continuous action in many of the illustrations. Halldor is not only one of world's top Nordic ski and ski jumping teachers and coaches, but also one of Norway's most noted artists. His artistic penchant for a new way to show a technique was of great help.

For our conditioning photos, we must thank our models Christian Arnessen and his wife, Sollaug. They own Norway's finest fitness center, the Kom i Form. Christian is one of Norway's greatest sportsmen, and one of his claims to fame is that he brought snowboarding to the country.

We owe a great debt of gratitude to many of the world's top skiers who are shown herein, as well as to Liv Arnesen and Cato Zahl Pedersen for lending us the photos of their treks to the South Pole and to Marit Sorensen for her photographic memory of her trip across Greenland.

Relative to the "care and feeding" of your skis, we must thank Harald Bjerke, Tor Willey and all of the other people at Swix who helped us with technical data on waxing; and Kenneth Aashein and Tomm Murstad Jr. of A/S Skiservice who brought us up to date on the most recent advances in ski base preparation and shared some secrets of the many world class skiers with whom they work.

And special thanks to all of the appropriate people at Masters Press: Tom Bast (the captain of the ship), Holly Kondras, Kathleen Prata, and Kim Heusel.

Disabled Sled Racer, Karl Seeman
The joy of gliding across the ice or snow can be enjoyed by nearly everyone.

Foreword

The thrill of sailing through a frozen landscape on a crisp clear day is what psychologist Abraham Maslow called a "peak experience" — the kind of experience which is truly meaningful in our lives. In Norway our national goal is often seen as skiing in our winter wonderland. We love our country and its incomparable beauty — and we like it best during the winter because we can ski everywhere in the country.

It seems that each snow-covered field and mountain has a beauty which every person can appreciate. But those of us who can ski through the woods and over the hills, across the lakes and down into the valleys, can appreciate it best. Our bodies are exhilarated while our minds are cleansed with nature's emollient.

I am personally delighted every time I observe or meet a beginning skier. I know how much joy is in store for that person. Whether in Norway, Italy or Austria, or California, Colorado or Vermont, the feeling of freedom is being experienced by all.

Sindre and Bob have provided you with the means to develop your technique, to learn to prepare your skis, to condition your body — and thereby enjoy to the utmost your skiing experience. I wish you well. And, we'd love to see you in Norway.

Erik Roste, Head Nordic ski coach and
Head men's coach for Norwegian National team

Cato Zahl Pedersen with friend crossing Antarctica —Cato has won 13 gold medals in three winter Para-Olympics in both downhill and cross country skiing and five more in sprints and distance running at two summer Para-Olympics. He lost both arms in an electrical accident many years agao. That sled he is pulling weighs several hundred pounds.

A Dual Preface

There is a common saying that Norwegians are born with skis on their feet. I guess that was the case with me. And for all of my 30 plus years I have enjoyed skiing. Whether it was playing as a child, racing as a teenager and young man, or coaching the world's best skiers, I have enjoyed every minute. Today my most relaxing times are when I step into my skis and skate through the woods. There is nothing like feeling the freedom of your body in the still white elegance of the forest.

Perhaps I should mention here that in Norway to *ga pa tur*, that is, take a tour together, is considered the universal elixir. In the United States, a doctor may tell you to "take two aspirin and call me in the morning," but in Norway the doctor's first advice for most mental and physical problems is to *ga pa tur*.

It is my deepest hope that you will be able to enjoy your skiing experience. And when you get to Norway, let's *ga pa tur*. In the meantime, good luck, or as we say *lykke til*.

Sindre Bergan

Marit Sorensen epitomizes the Norwegian attitude that skiing is a way of life. When Marit was working hard on completing her doctorate in psychology, doing her research and writing was the most important thing in her life. Of course her primary goal was number one only after she had skied two or three hours a day — and perhaps ridden her horse for an hour or so.

It was Marit's concept that "skiing is a way of life" which opened up to me the idea that there is more than the ultimate physical workout of cross country skiing and the intimacy it allows with the joys of winter. Skiing offers the opportunity for self-expression, for rhythm of movement, for self-reflection and for challenge.

Marit Sorensen

The challenge of the snow has led Norwegian after Norwegian to gold medal performances in all types of skiing. It has led many Norwegians to be the first in challenging the frozen tundra of the North and South poles. Fridtjof Nansen, in 1895, went the farthest north that anyone had ever gone, being less than 4 degrees from the North Pole. Roald Amundsen discovered the South Pole in 1911 and was the first person to see both poles. That same challenge led Marit Sorensen to lead the first all-woman expedition across Greenland in 1990, and it led Cato Zahl Pedersen to ski to the South Pole without arms — arms which had been lost in an accident 20 years before.

Whether you answer the challenge of a race, the call of the unconquered, the beckoning of nature's beauty, or the enjoyment of the most effective type of physical exercise — you will enjoy your skiing experience.

Bob O'Connor

Cross Country Skiing

1

Introduction to Nordic Cross Country Skiing

When we think of cross country skiing — Nordic skiing — we think of Norway. The sparsely populated country of only four million people not only gave birth to the sport, but has dominated it in international competitions since they were first begun.

It is said that Norwegians are born with skis on their feet. While this may be a bit of an exaggeration, it is close to the truth. Infants are carried on the backs of their parents as they ski, or they are pulled in small sleds (pulks) behind one of the parents. It is not uncommon to see a father pulling an infant sled at the end of a 10-foot harness — then behind that sled is a small child's sled to be used by the child when the parents stop for a picnic along a trail.

Throughout the country there are machine-made trails which the skiers can follow for miles and miles. But the regal ranges of mountains and valleys beckon the intermediate skier to trek into the virgin snow which mantles the entire nation. In Oslo, the capital city, people ski on the streets and over the golf courses, but generally they find their ways to the top of the city and the great north woods (Nordmarka). Here at the last tram stop you can ski the prepared tracks, take off

A Family Skiing Outing in Norway

over the frozen lakes and pine-covered hills, or skate the advanced trails. And with the many miles of lighted trails, you can ski all night long if you so desire.

Whether you are skiing the open terrain under the canopy of sky or clouds, or passing beneath the crystal coated arches of the ice glazed pines or birches, the freedom of skis brings you closer to nature. It enthralls your soul with the frozen magnificence of winter's wonders.

Ah! But there's more to skiing than communing with nature. Cross country skiing is the finest aerobic exercise you can experience. It is better than running, swimming or cycling. It uses the muscles of the upper and lower body. It is a complete exercise and recognized by the leading fitness experts as the ultimate method for body conditioning.

Even disabled skiers at every age enjoy the freedom of the sport, whether skiing on a sled or a "walker" mounted on skis.

And as a hobby which the whole family can enjoy, there is no better activity than cross country skiing. Do you want competition? There are races. Do you want to ski, then shoot at targets? Try the biathlon. How about orienteering? In this activity you compete with compass and maps using your body and your wits to enjoy the day in the snow. Nordic skiing offers the complete spectrum of activities from recreation to competition.

There's plenty of adventure to be had on skis. And Norwegians have led the way. How about traveling alone to the South Pole? Liv Arnesen did it in 1995 —

A biathlete skis then shoots at a target. It is an Olympic event.

Liv Arnesen's Adventure —
Cross Country Skiing to the
South Pole

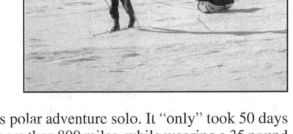

the first woman to accomplish this polar adventure solo. It "only" took 50 days on the polar ice cap for her to ski more than 800 miles, while wearing a 35 pound backpack and pulling a sled weighing 85 kilograms (185 pounds). Liv, by the way, is the lady on both the front and back covers.

So Nordic skiing — cross country skiing — can be whatever you want it to be — exercise, a union with nature, a source for competition or a vehicle to the ultimate in physical challenges. What do you want it to be for you? It is now "Your Sport."

About This Book

The chapters are written so that they can stand alone. You can therefore start wherever you want. If you are interested in equipment first, start there. If you want to understand the mechanics of skiing so that you can be more aware of why you should choose the equipment you want, start with the mechanics chapter. If you think that you want to learn the classic technique of traditional skiing, start there. But if you have had experience in ice skating or roller skating and think you can learn a skating technique easier, start with the skating chapter. Whichever approach you take, when you have read the whole book you will have a pretty good idea of the sport — and the experience — which is much more than a sport.

We are giving you the basics in technique. Your technique will change with the snow conditions, the slope of the hill, your speed and your own feelings of competence. There is no "one way" to ski. You are an individual and you will ski as an individual. It won't be long before your friends will be able to spot you from a half mile away and say "there's old Christie" or "Well, look at James over there." Your style will be distinctive, and the real you will show through.

If your body is in good shape from aerobics, running or swimming, you may not need any extra physical conditioning. But if you have been a couch potato or a video nut you may want to prepare your body just a little. Look at the conditioning chapter early in your reading.

Balance is essential, because you should always be gliding on only one ski. That means you must have "one foot balance." We have given you some exercises for this. It is really much easier to spend five minutes a day for a few days increasing your balance ability than to try it first on the snow.

So if you have the time and the inclination, spend a week or two getting ready before your first ski tour. If you don't have the time beforehand — just hit the snow and have a ball! (A snow ball?)

Also don't worry about equipment early on. Borrow it, or better yet, rent it. Just be sure that your hands stay warm. Your feet won't be a problem. They are usually toasty in their wool socks and leather boots.

Be ready to have fun! Four million Norwegians can't be wrong. The only thing on which they all agree is that "Skiing is Fun!"

4

2

A Little Practice Before You Ski

Balance: The Key to Skiing

Some people say that skiing is like walking — but it is really more like roller skating. You push and you glide. You transfer weight from one ski to the other. How can you get both push and glide from the same ski? That is done by proper waxing techniques which will be explained later.

For now it is enough to know that you push and glide. You push with a pole and your leg, while you glide on the other leg. Simple! It just takes a little practice.

When you ski, you glide — and gliding requires balance. That balance comes from a number of factors. The fluid in your inner ears is a major factor. As you move forward or backward, or side to side, the fluid in the three semicircular canals of the inner ear signals your brain to adjust your muscle tension in the hips, legs, back, arms, etc. So the more you weave back and forth, the more signals your brain must send, and the more often your different muscles will have to contract to maintain your balance. As you become smoother, with less side-to-side motion in your skiing, there will be fewer signals for the brain to react to and fewer adjustments as well. So as your balance improves, your skiing improves — and as your skiing improves, your balance improves.

The eyes also play a part in your balance. Try closing one or both eyes and you will find it more difficult to balance. A common test that police give to suspected drunks is to have them close their eyes, then, with extended arms, try to touch their index fingers together. Not being able to see greatly reduces your ability to coordinate and balance.

Pressure on your feet or tension in your hips or legs also signals the body to make balance adjustments. As weight is shifted to one foot and you fall off balance outwardly, your brain signals the muscles on the inside of that leg to tense up, and you are pulled back to a balanced position. If you didn't quite get enough weight on that leg you would tend to fall inward, so the muscles on the outside of your lower leg and thigh tense up and pull you to a balanced position. This kind of balancing from one leg to the other occurs whenever we stand.

Balance is actually the shifting of your center of gravity over your base. The center of gravity is that point in your body which is the exact center of your weight. It is in the center of your hips. The exact location depends on where you carry the most weight. For this reason women generally have a center of gravity slightly lower in their hips than do men. A person with heavier legs will have a lower center of gravity while a person with a heavier upper body will have a higher center of gravity.

Shorter people have centers of gravity closer to the ground so their balance should be easier. Taller people will have more problems because their center of gravity will be farther away from their base — their feet.

For example, the center of gravity of a "seesaw" or "teeter-totter" would be in the exact middle of the board. If two equally weighted children sit on opposite sides of the board, the center of gravity is maintained and each can easily push off and ride up and down. If, however, a 50-pound child sits on one end and a 60-pound child on the other, the board will not move effectively because the center of gravity of the board will have moved toward the heavier child. So to bring the center of gravity back to the middle of the board, the heavier child will have to move closer to the middle of the board until the center of gravity is again in the middle, and the children can easily move up and down with only a slight push.

Your center of gravity shifts right or left, forward or backward, as your body bends or your legs shift. If you bend at the waist 90 degrees, you will notice that your hips move backward and are no longer over the feet. But remember your center of gravity is over your feet; if it weren't, you would fall. So your balance must constantly adjust to the shifting center of gravity. And if that center of gravity moves outside of your base (your feet), you will fall — unless you can catch your balance by putting a pole down, by moving your arms to shift the center of gravity, or by shifting your weight on to the other ski.

To increase your balancing ability, it is best to practice balance exercises before you start to ski. However, if you have done a great deal of roller skating or ice skating, your balance may already be quite good, and you may be ready to hop on your new skis and hit the trail.

Improving Your Balance Before You Ski

If you are a beginner whose balance is questionable, you can practice at home without skis.

1) Stand on one leg, and balance as long as you can. Move to the other leg, and hold your balance as long as possible.

2) Hop sideways from one foot to the other. Hold your balance on one leg as long as you can, then hop to the other leg and hold your balance.

3) When you can do that easily, hop forward 6 to 10 inches on each hop. Then increase your hop distance and increase your balancing time on each foot.

4) Close your eyes and balance on both legs. Then do the same on the right leg, then the left leg.

On the Snow

You will need to get comfortable on your skis. Put them on. If the binding doesn't snap readily, check it to see that there is no snow or dirt in the binding or on your boot. If there is, clean it out and try again.

Now put your hand through the pole strap by bringing your hand upward through the strap. Bring your thumb and forefinger down on the pole grip. There should be little play in the strap because you want the strap to hold your hand comfortably close to the grip.

When you push on your pole to help propel you forward, there will be pressure on both your grip and on your strap. When you finish the push, you will relax your hand as you swing the pole forward. When you are ready to grip the pole again, the strap will have held the grip close to your hand. You will not keep a tight grip on your pole throughout your stride. You will grip as you push, then relax. If you kept a tight grip on the pole continuously, your forearms would be tense and might cramp. While skiing, you want your arms and legs to be as relaxed as possible.

Here are some drills to get used to being on skis and on the snow.

1) Try double poling and gliding. Extend your arms forward, plant the pole tips about even with your feet and not too wide. Then push with both arms. Feel the glide. Do it again. If you are skiing in tracks that have already been prepared, you will find it quite easy. Your balance will be easier to maintain because you will have a wider base of support.

2) Again, extend your arms in front of you, plant your poles about even with your feet. Now bend at the waist and push back with your arms. You will feel even more power and will be able to glide farther.

3) While standing, lift one ski off the snow and balance. Then lift the other. See how long you can balance.

4) With your feet even, push back on the right pole and glide, then push on the left pole and glide. Do this until you feel comfortable and relaxed, swinging one arm forward as you push back with the other arm. Get a rhythm — right, glide, left, glide.

5) Without using your poles, jog on your skis. Take very short steps, and bounce along the trail. Bend your arms at the elbows, just as if you were jogging. The quick jogging steps will not require you to use much balance, but they will get your arms and legs coordinated with your right hand and left knee work-

ing together then your left hand and right knee. Don't even think about the coordination. If you can walk, your coordination will be fine. You just want to get the feeling of shifting your weight with skis on.

When you feel comfortable with balancing on one leg while standing and balancing on both legs while moving with the double pole push and glide, you are ready to try classical skiing or skating. This is where you will find that either style is almost like roller skating or ice skating.

Should you fall before you have finished the book, just get your skis under you and stand up. You can't stand up with your skis to the side. But, of course, after you have completed the book you will never fall. You will have mastered the proper techniques and will have perfect balance. Once the snow realizes this it will never trip you up. (Pity the poor people who read other books. You'll see them falling everywhere!)

The Skills

1) Balancing on one leg.
2) Balancing alternately, one leg then the other.
3) Gliding on both skis.
4) Double poling — planting and pushing off both poles at the same time.
5) Single poling — alternately planting the right pole, then the left and pushing off the planted pole.
6) Jogging on skis.

3

Diagonal Striding and Classic Skiing

Learning the Traditional Method of Skiing

Classical skiing is the diagonal striding technique which fascinates us with the sport. It is a combination of walking and roller skating or ice skating. You push off on one leg and glide on the other. Of course, your arms will help a lot. Instead of just swinging them as in walking or skating, you push backward as you do in swimming. This makes classical skiing the best type of aerobic workout. It has the advantages of walking or running and swimming simultaneously. Add to this the fact that you are experiencing this activity in the great outdoors, and you have the ultimate sport — a combination of dynamic exercise with the aesthetic feeling of waltzing in a winter wonderland.

Getting the Feel of Gliding

It is the gliding which gives skiing that special feeling which you can't get while running. Let us review how to glide with the double pole push. With your weight on both skis, bring both arms forward. Plant the pole tips into the snow with the tips behind the hands. Push backward and downward with the arms. Then glide to a stop. Repeat this until you feel comfortable with the push back and glide.

Next, start with the same action, but as you push downward, bend at the waist letting your abdominal muscles work. Your power will now come from the abdominal muscles, the muscles of the upper sides of the back (latissimus dorsi) and the back of the upper arms (triceps). We will come back to this skill at the intermediate level.

Beginning to Ski

You develop the power by the push of one leg and the poling action of the opposite arm. The right leg and left arm work together, just like in walking. You may start your first diagonal striding by simply walking with short steps to get the feeling of walking on skis. If you are lucky enough to have a machine-prepared trail, it will be easy because the tracks keep your skis in line and at the proper distance apart. If you must go it alone on flat snow, you may find that your skis want to separate. Just put a little more tension on the muscles on the inside of your leg and you'll be fine.

In the first photo notice the slight C curve of the spine as the right leg reaches out and glides. In the middle photo the legs are closer together and the spine is straight. In the third photo the C curve is reversed as the weight is on the left ski.

Once you get the feeling of sliding on the snow, try to get a little glide. Push with the pole and leg, and glide on the forward ski. When you feel comfortable with a little glide, you will be ready to emphasize the push or "kick" with your power leg. Keep in mind, however, that if you don't use your kick to extend your glide, there is no reason for pushing! The glide is what it is all about.

One very important point to remember in all of your skiing is to bend your ankle. When your ankle bends, your knee bends. And when your knee bends, your hips bend. A major problem with beginning skiers is that they keep their legs too stiff.

The poles should be held loosely. The hand goes up through the pole strap then comes down on the handle. (See photos on the following page.) With this grip, the power of the arm swing can be transferred by a combination of pres-

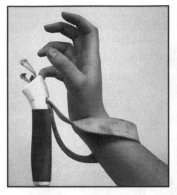 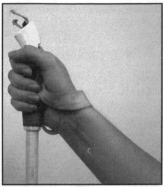

The skier should put his or her arm upward through the strap on the pole. Don't grip it too tightly in order to avoid tension and fatigue in the hand and forearm.

sures of the hand against the handle and the wrist against the strap. The poles should be gripped loosely except for the power phase of the downward push. Gripping the pole too tightly can increase the tension and fatigue the hand and forearm.

The Force Phase, or "kick" phase of the stride, occurs when weight is applied to the forward ski, and friction is developed under the center of the ski. At this point while your leg is moving backward, the ski should be motionless as the waxed area in the middle of the ski grips the snow and pushes against it. This phase will take about a third of a second. The beginning of the force phase of the stride occurs just as the gliding ski is pulled back and the foot is directly under the body. This happens when the rear ski is passing the front (gliding) ski.

If you have trouble coordinating your arms and legs, forget the poles for a while and just concentrate on pushing off with your foot. If you can find a slight downward incline, it will be much easier because each push will allow you a longer glide. All of your weight should be on the kicking ski. This allows you to press the waxed part of the ski into the snow and to get the maximum push. If your power leg slips backward when you push, you either do not have enough

Kicking Force: *Notice the kicking force with the fully extended left leg and the reaching glide of the right leg.*

11

Planting the Pole Early: *Get the pole planted early near the toe of the boot.*

weight on it for your kick or, if you are wearing waxed skis, the wax is not right for the snow. More about that in the chapter on waxing.

The Pole Push is extremely important. Beginners often plant the pole too early for balance, and push too little. The pole tip will be planted near the toe of your boot or a bit farther back. If you use longer poles, the plant will be even farther back. If you are going uphill, the plant will also be farther back.

Double Pole and Glide: *As a beginner, get the feeling of pushing with your poles then gliding as long as you can. Notice that the eyes are looking forward, not down. See also that the arms stay in an arc which is close to and parallel with the side of the body.*

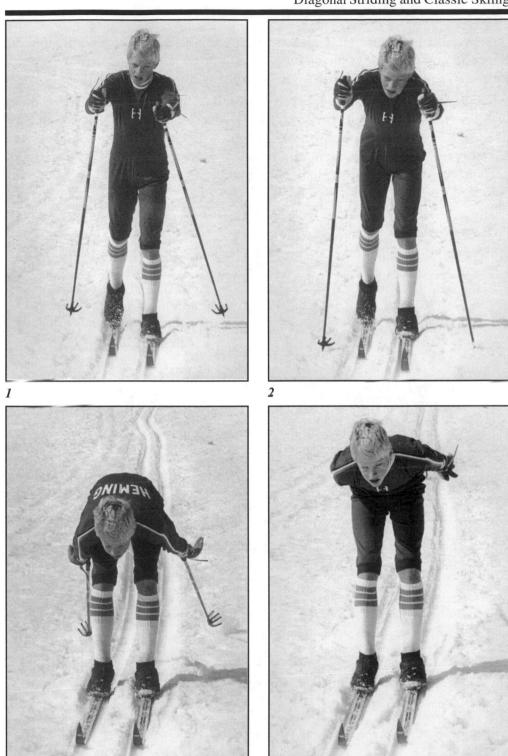

1

2

3

4

Double pole with the body bent: *Snorre Krogstad plants the poles near the toes, takes a full bend at the waist and proceeds with a full follow-through.*

As you get comfortable on your skis, work on a quicker pole plant and a long and powerful push. Plant your pole as soon as your hand reaches forward. Push down and backward with force. As you do this, your grip will change.

When your arm swings forward, you will "catch" the pole grip. You don't want to grip too hard, because it will be the strap which will be your major connection with the pole. If your grip is too tight, you will tense the muscles in your forearm and reduce the amount of relaxation which you want. So you will start with a firm (not tight) grip on the pole, but as the pole is pushed backward the

Former world junior champion Hanne Krogstad demonstrates a side view of the double pole plant. She plants the poles near the toes (left), then shows the full arm extension and release of the grip at the end of the pole push (below).

grip is relaxed and more of the force of your swing is transmitted through your pole straps. When you have finished your push, your arm and pole will be in nearly a straight line. You can't keep the same grip on the pole as you did at the beginning of the action when the arm was at a nearly 90 degree angle to the pole.

To aid in the transmission of the power from the hand to the pole, some skiers will tighten the strap so that the pole grip stays closer to the hand. Others will finish the push with a tighter thumb-index finger grip on the pole. Whichever method you choose, keep in mind that at the end of your arm stroke, the pole will be closer to the horizontal position so more of your force is being transmitted effectively in the direction that you are skiing. But at the beginning of the arm stroke the pole is nearly vertical to the snow, so most of the power pushes upward and lifts the body. The farther back the pole is pushed, the more horizontal power is generated and less vertical power. Consequently, the longer your stroke, the more efficient it is in developing power and speed.

At the instant you plant your pole, your arm will be bent. Having a bent arm gives you a shorter radius from shoulder to hand. This makes it easier for your upper back and shoulder muscles to work effectively. It takes only one-quarter of the force to generate the same speed if your arm is bent at 90 degrees as it would if your arm were completely straight. However, your arm will be flexed only 30 to 45 degrees. (Racers will have a much greater angle at the elbow so that they can more forcefully extend their arms at the end of the poling action.)

Your initial force will come from your upper back (latissimus dorsi), rear shoulder (posterior deltoid) and back of the upper arm (triceps). If your arm were straight throughout the stroke, you would not be able to generate power from a large part of the triceps. But with the bent arm, you will generate more power during the final extension of your arm.

Stride Length is a major factor in skiing efficiency. Generally, the harder you push the longer you can glide. This relationship holds true at every level — from beginners to Olympians. Keep working on lengthening the stride by increasing your glide.

Diagonal Stride: *Be certain to glide on only one ski at a time.*

Diagonal Stride

The problem most often encountered here is the lack of one-legged balance. If you are having problems here, go back to the one-legged balance drills at home or on the snow. It may take a while to train the muscles on the inside and outside of your hips, thighs and ankles to correctly hold your body in the one-legged position. One-legged balance is critical to every phase of cross country skiing.

When you begin skiing, your strides will be short. Just concentrate on shifting your weight smoothly from one ski to the other. This will give you the feel of skiing. The balance will come if you are working on the one-legged balance exercises. As you learn to push off more forcefully, your gliding ski will be pushed forward more and your glide will be naturally increased. Classical skiing requires long leg strides and long arm swings.

Meanwhile, be sure that you keep your skis on the snow. Beginners often attempt to "walk" and lift the ski. This is not only inefficient, but it can ice up the ski bottoms. The snow on the bottom of the skis melts and then refreezes as it is exposed to the freezing air.

Concentrate on the glide. The push will generally take care of itself. Lean forward as if you are leaning into a stiff breeze. Your torso will be bent forward at about 45 degrees. Your chest will be nearly over your knee, and your ankle will be under your knee. Your thigh will be at an angle of 30 to 45 degrees from the vertical, and your weight will be on your heel. If you were to put weight on your toes, more of your waxed kicking area would come in contact with the snow and slow you down. Naturally, you don't want your kick wax hitting the snow when you are gliding.

Intermediate Skills

Once you feel comfortable with the diagonal stride and the alternating arm coordination, as well as feeling the power of the arms and legs as you glide, you are ready for more intermediate skills. Be patient about moving to the intermedi-

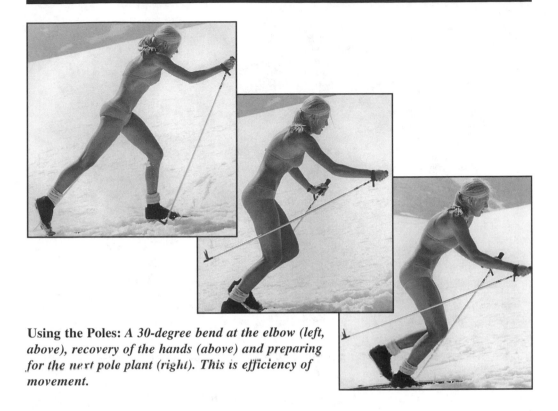

Using the Poles: *A 30-degree bend at the elbow (left, above), recovery of the hands (above) and preparing for the next pole plant (right). This is efficiency of movement.*

Keep head bobbing to a minimum. Some up-and-down movement is unavoidable but excessive movement is counterproductive.

***Former world champion Annette Bøe: Notice how her gliding hip moves forward as the
kicking leg fully extends.***

ate level. It will probably take several sessions of practice before you feel comfortable.

Throwing the gliding hip forward is a technique that the better skiers use.
By reaching aggressively with the leading hip, your stride can be increased. The
strong kick backwards with the other leg should also pull that hip backward. The
result is complete use of the hips.

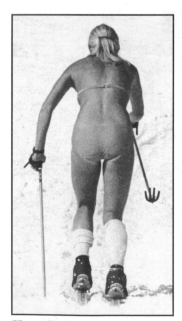

***Hane Krogstad demonstrates the diagonal stride from the rear. Notice the weight shift to
the left leg as she glides on that leg in the photo at far right.***

Top view of the diagonal stride: *Notice the glide on the left leg in the second photo as the leg finishes its kick. Note that the body angle and the angle of the pole at the instant of plant are about the same.*

Beginners tend to keep the hips perpendicular to the line of travel. This is caused by the lack of a forceful push and the restricted forward movement of the gliding leg. This is a major difference between the beginner and the more advanced skier. Once you feel comfortable with the diagonal striding and can balance effectively, the next skill to learn is a powerful hip rotation. Such a rotation is not done in running because running does not have a glide phase. So it is a movement which must be learned specifically for skiing.

The proper hip thrust forces you to get your body farther over your gliding ski. This should force your torso forward and bring more weight over the gliding ski.

Keeping the kicking leg slightly bent as it moves under the hips allows for a faster thrust of the leg (because of the shorter radius from the hip to the foot) and allows for the leg to extend powerfully at the end of the kick. Beginners often keep their legs straight and stiff during the kick. The more advanced skiers understand the power of propulsion from the bent leg and utilize it in their stride.

Double poling is a very efficient technique to use with the diagonal stride of classic skiing. As you move into the intermediate level of skiing, you may want to consider double poling at times. The technique is aided by longer poles which allow force to be transmitted with a better angle. Longer poles and bending at the waist allow the skier to direct more force horizontally which results in more speed.

Marja Liisa Kirvesniemi, an Olympic champion, demonstrates an initial pole plant with the angle of the elbow at 30 to 40 degrees at the moment of plant.

Thomas Wassberg, above, was the first of the great racers to use an elbow bend of greater than 90 degrees. Notice the force generated through the poles as the poles are bending under the force of the push back.

    The poles are planted farther back which gives a flatter angle with more of the push being forward than upward. It also reduces the friction from the air (aerodynamic drag) by up to 20 percent because the body bends dynamically at the waist during the poling phase of the stride.

    To pole with a kick, kick first, then immediately double pole, then glide on both skis. The kicking leg will recover as you begin your double pole movement backward. Be sure to let your body weight provide most of the pole power. It is the bending at the waist, not the push back of the arms, which should provide most of the power. You will first bend powerfully at the waist, using your abdominal muscles, then extend your arms backward.

Marja Liisa Kirvesniemi demonstrates the pole plant ready to be made near the toes.

Raisa Smetanina demonstrates a full sequence of the kick, double pole technique.

Berit Aunli illustrates the double pole plant just after the kick phase is completed.

21

Changing from diagonal striding to the double pole and kick is a skill which should be mastered. Terrain conditions or fatigue may require a change of poling for maximum efficiency. To change from diagonal striding, you can leave one arm forward while the other arm recovers and moves forward. Now with both arms forward you are ready for a double poling thrust. Another method is to leave one arm back until the other arm completes its push, then bring both arms forward together. Try both methods to see which is more comfortable for you.

To change from double poling to single poling, you can leave one arm back when the double poling thrust is completed. Then move one arm forward as the opposite leg moves forward, and you are diagonal striding again.

Ski your own way after you have mastered the basic techniques. Some people have powerful arms and will emphasize the arm push. Swimmers and gymnasts are likely to have such power. Others use their kick as the major propulsive force. Runners and those whose former sports interests included running, such as basketball or football, will often rely heavily on the kick. Old injuries may play a part in how you ski. Ankle, knee or back injuries may affect your ability to flex those joints. Also, injuries may reduce your ability to push backward.

Checklist

Force or Push Off

1) Hips over your feet.

2) Upper body leans slightly forward.

3) Feet parallel, with both feet under your body.

4) Legs are flexed at the knee.

5) Lift one arm forward; plant the pole with the tip near your toes.

6) Push back with the arm while kicking back with the opposite leg.

Gliding

1) Upper body leans forward.

2) Eyes look ahead, not down at the skis.

3) Weight shifts completely from the kicking ski to the other ski — the gliding ski.

4) The arm opposite the gliding ski swings forward.

Common Problems

1) Using poles for balance — To corect this, keep them out to the side of the body, instead of pushing with them. Drop the poles and let your arms swing naturally as if you were walking or running.

2) Poor coordination of arms and legs — Drop the poles and let the arms work naturally. Or, drop the poles and jog on your skis, taking short, quick steps.

Let your arms work as they would if you were jogging.

3) No glide because the weight isn't transferred to the gliding ski since the weight is kept on both skis for better balance — Stop and lift one leg and balance, then lift the other leg and balance. Begin again, emphasizing the one-legged balance as you glide.

4) Your kicking ski slips — Stand more upright with the hips forward and the torso forward. Are you transferring all of your weight to the push off ski? Check your wax. It may be the wrong wax or it may not be thick enough. (See Chapter 10.)

5) Your skis hit the snow early and make a slapping sound — Your upper body is not far enough forward so that your trailing ski hits the snow before your foot is under your hips.

Skill Improvement Drills

Beginner

1) Find a flat area then walk on the skis without poles. Swing the arms straight forward and backward. The hands should not cross over the skis.

2) Jog with very short steps without poles.

3) Push with both poles and glide.

4) Try all of the above on a slight downward slope so that gliding is easier.

Intermediate

If your double poling is not as effective as it might be, it may be wise to:

1) Check to see that you are not squatting (bending your knees too much) when you bend at the waist.

2) Check also to see that your upper body is bent nearly 90 degrees at the waist. It is the weight of the upper body, not the arm strength, which is the key to arm power.

3) Accent the push backward with the arms as the final thrust of the movement.

4

Going Up Hills

Going up hills is an essential part of cross country skiing. The techniques are quite simple to learn. The problem is that it uses much more energy than going downhill. As a beginner, you may be led to believe that the course is 98 percent uphill with the two percent downhill being in a straight drop. Of course, that isn't quite true — except in Norway! The usual downhill run is only a 45-degree slope! Well, not quite.

As with every other aspect of Nordic skiing, there are beginner, intermediate and advanced techniques. We will look at the beginner and intermediate techniques in this chapter while the advanced methods are included in the chapter on skating.

Beginner Techniques

Both the side step and the herringbone, or as the Norwegians call it, the "fish bone," are beginner techniques which all skiers will use sometimes. The conditions which determine when they will be used by the more advanced skiers are the degree of the slope of the hill or the condition of the snow, such as the amount of ice.

You do the **side step** by getting your skis across the "fall line." That is, get your skis exactly perpendicular to the slope of the hill. Keep your body erect, your head up and your poles outside of your skis. From this position bend your knees slightly and move them toward the slope of the hill. As your knees move toward the hill, your ankles, boots and skis will also tilt toward the hill.

The movement of the boot pushes the uphill edge of the ski into the snow and lifts the downhill edge of the ski. The ski is now "edged" into the snow so

Side Step

that it bites into the snow. The steeper the angle of the slope of the hills, the more "edge" you will need to keep the skis from sliding down the hill. Take small steps at first to get the feel of the edged ski. Lift the uphill ski 6 to 10 inches up the fall line, then bring the other ski up to it. Keep repeating this movement as you climb the hill.

Use your poles for balance, especially the downhill pole which can be used for an extra push off as the uphill ski is moved up the hill. Also use that pole to stabilize your body as your downhill ski is brought up to the higher ski. Keep your body erect, your head up and your poles outside of your skis.

Edging the ski into the snow

If your skis begin to slip sideways, you don't have enough edge into the hill. Just bend the knees more into the slope. If your ski tips or tails begin to slide downward, you have moved away from the fall line. Find the fall line again. If your tips were slipping downward, they are closer to the fall line so move toward them. If your tails were slipping, move them up the hill and move toward them.

Note: Very few hills have a perfectly consistent fall line. Every bump of snow, every mogul and every rock can change the fall line.

While beginners may use this technique on many hills, the advanced skiers use it only on the steepest hills or on very slippery ice. Since the side-stepping technique is used for climbing any kind of hill, you should learn to be comfortable with it early in your career. Learn to do it with your left side to the hill and with your right side toward the hill.

The **herringbone** obviously gets its name from the type of tracks it leaves in the snow. They look like the bones of a fish seen from behind the backbone — sort of a gourmet's eye view after you have boned the trout.

The Herringbone

It is easiest to start on flat land. Move your ski tips outward while keeping the tails close together. Your skis will now form a "V." Walk forward a few steps while using the poles to help to push you.

Now start up the hill. Keep the same V position of the skis with your poles outside of the skis. As you begin to go up the hill, bring your knees and ankles inward to edge the inside of the ski which is on the snow. This will prevent you from going backward. There is nothing magic about the V position of the skis if they are flat on the snow. You will still slide backward unless they are edged.

27

Stand upright and keep your head up. This will help to keep your weight centered over your boots. Bending forward shifts your weight back toward your heels. Take reasonably large steps. The shallower the slope, the longer the steps you can take. Use your poles just as if you are walking, with the right arm swinging forward while the left leg moves up the hill. Be sure to plant the pole well behind your hands so that it is angled backward. This way it can be used effectively to push.

If you start to slip backward, widen the V of your skis and edge in the ski on which you have your weight. Do that by bringing the knee inward on the ski which you are edging. Then use your poles, exerting more push on each step.

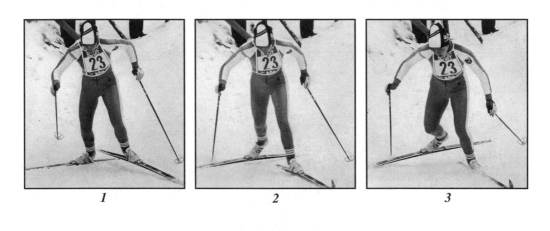

1   2   3

4   5

A front view of the herring-bone. On this steep hill, notice the wide angle of the skis.

Poling becomes quicker and stronger as you go uphill. The steeper the hill and the less the skill, the more strides will be taken per minute. Consequently, the more frequent will be your pole plants. The poles will also be planted farther back to propel you up the hill. Since quicker poling action will be taken, the arms will be bent more. The shorter the radius from your shoulder to your hand, the more power you can generate from your shoulder and arm muscles. So, the steeper the hill, the greater the elbow bend and the quicker the poling action.

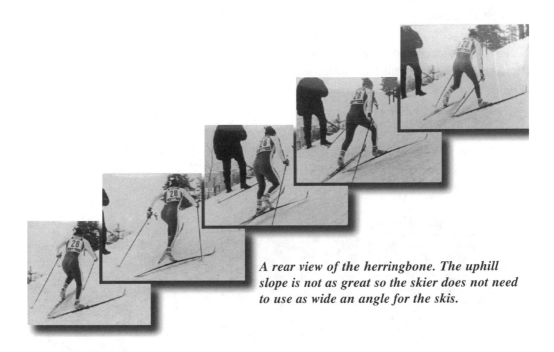

A rear view of the herringbone. The uphill slope is not as great so the skier does not need to use as wide an angle for the skis.

In another front view of the herringbone, the slope of the hill is so slight that the skier can keep his skis nearly parallel.

Still greater force can be exerted if you use your abdominal muscles, along with gravity, to force the poles downward. Your shoulder muscles will merely hold your poles steady while the abdominals start the downward movement of the poles. Then, when the abdominals have exerted their force, the shoulder muscles and the triceps continue to push the poles backward.

The Diagonal Stride

When you are able to approach the hill with more speed, you can continue your diagonal striding up the hill. If you can do this, it is much easier than using the herringbone steps.

Using the diagonal stride on a slight uphill path.

To stride up the hill, you must aggressively transfer all of your weight to the force ski, the kicking ski. You want to be able to get the wax pocket, or the kicking area of the ski, completely into the snow so that you can get the maximum amount of friction possible. You will also want to lean with your hips forward. You must be certain that you are not leaning too far forward or your hips will be pushed too far back in order to maintain your balance. If your hips are too far back, your skis will slip. Keep your hips forward.

Naturally, your poling will also be harder than when skiing the flats. You will not push as far back as you do when skiing on a level trail, because your arms and legs will be moving quicker to keep your speed up the hill. When we discuss skating up hills in Chapter 7, you will have other options for moving up hills effectively.

1   *2*

Kristen Skjeldal, 1991 World Cup gold medalist and a member of the 1992 Olympic championship relay team, demonstrates the Paddle dance uphill. Note the body weight shift and the head position. (See Chapter 7 for technique.)

Checklist

1) Keep your gliding knee over your foot. If your gliding foot gets ahead of your knee, you will lose power because your hips will be forced backward.

2) Keep the angle at your ankle, about 90 degrees. If the knee gets too far ahead of your foot, your hips will tend to move up and down, and you will lose power.

3) Reach forward with the gliding hip to increase your glide uphill.

5

Going Down Hills

You can be certain that you will be doing some downhill skiing on your tour unless the course is perfectly flat. For every hill you go up, there is a hill to go down. If you were to ski in an international race, you would be assured that at least a third of the course would be downhill.

Downhill skiing gives you the feeling of flying, with the wind whipping through your hair and bathing your face. If you are a recreational skier, you can use this downhill run for resting, or you can enjoy the rush of a "shush" for its excitement. If you are a racer you will want to add even more speed and pick up more time against your competition. But let's start with the most basic skills.

Side Slipping

A very important skill to learn is the side slip. To do this, stand on a hill with your skis across the fall line. Move your knees and ankles toward the downhill side. The skis should begin to slip downhill. To stop, move the knees and ankles inward toward the uphill side.

Once comfortable with side slipping and stopping at a right angle to the skis, try side slipping forward and backward. To side slip in the forward direction, lean your weight forward so that more weight is on the toes, move the knees and ankles toward the direction you want to move, and flatten your skis on the snow. To side slip backward, put your weight on your heels, slip into a position in which your heels point in the direction you want to move, and flatten the skis on the snow.

The sideslip technique should be mastered, because it is essential for very steep inclines and for icy conditions. It will give the beginner great confidence in any type of terrain. Even the expert may need to side slip forward and backward when moving down a treacherous slope which is either steep or icy, or both. If you don't learn to side slip, you may have to spend the rest of the winter on some steep icy crevasse — just you and the polar bears.

The Wedge (Snow Plow)

The most important technique to learn for beginners is the wedge. It is used at all levels of skiing.

The wedge is used at all levels of skiing

To execute the wedge:

1) With the legs fairly straight, push the heels outward and the toes inward. The front tips of the skis can be as much as 12 inches (30 cm) apart.

2) The upper body bends slightly forward at the hips.

3) More weight is put on the heels to allow for pushing the heels outward to control the tails of the skis.

4) The poles can be tucked under the arms.

To control the speed or to stop, bring the knees inward. This edges the skis and creates more friction. Simultaneously, increase the angles of the skis by pushing the tails outward or by bringing the tips inward.

To move faster down the hill, move the knees outward to flatten the skis on the snow.

For turning while in the wedge position, see Chapter 6.

Notice that the outside edges of the skis are up. This "edges" the inside edges of the skis and "applies the breaks" so you can stop.

The Half Wedge

The half wedge is handy when you are skiing in tracks and going downhill. If you want to slow down, just bring one ski out of the track and put it into the wedge position. The ski in the track will keep you in the proper path. The wedged ski will allow you to slow as much as you want by widening it or by edging it.

Following the Fall Line

Skiing straight down the hill is really quite simple — especially in tracks. Just lean your body a bit forward so that your knees are forward of your ankles. Increasing the bend at the knees lowers your center of gravity (the spot where your weight is concentrated — in the middle of your hips) and makes you more stable. Have your weight equally balanced on both skis.

As you ski down the hill in this "tuck" position, try to keep your center of gravity (in your hips) parallel to the snow. That is, try to keep your hips the same distance from the general slope of the hill all the time. You will be skiing with your knees slightly bent. If you come to a bump, bend your knees more to absorb the shock. If there is a little dip, extend your legs so that your hips stay as close to parallel with the angle of the hill as is possible. It is essential to stay relaxed and flexible.

If you really want to go fast, make yourself into an egg — that's a yolk! You will have to bend forward to decrease wind resistance. The ultimate position is what we call the "egg" shape which is very aerodynamic.

Skiing Across the Fall Line (Traversing)

In skiing across the mountain, you will need a slightly different technique. Obviously one ski will be higher on the hill than the other. The uphill ski will be slightly advanced of the downhill ski. This will happen naturally if you turn your body slightly down the hill. Having one leg forward will give you better balance.

Skiing across the fall line

Most of your weight will be on the trailing downhill ski. Try to keep the skis flat on the snow without edging them. This is done by moving the ankles slightly outward toward the downhill side. If, however, the snow is icy or you are going fast, you may need to edge the skis by bringing the knees and ankles inward toward the top of the hill.

Tuck Position

Egg Position

The Traversing Side Slip

You may want to move farther down the hill when traversing. This can be accomplished by adding a side slip to your forward traversing direction. During your traverse, move your knees more outward and point the toes more downhill than when you are merely traversing. Flatten the skis on the snow and begin sliding at a sharper angle downhill.

If you begin to go too fast, just bring your knees closer to the upward slope of the hill and your skis will edge. If you want to go still slower, turn up the hill.

Skiing Downhill

For most people, skiing downhill is the most exciting aspect of skiing. In order to make it the most enjoyable, you must practice, practice, practice. And your major achievement must be balance, balance, balance. A key ingredient in your ability to ski downhill fast is how much courage you have. This is just as true for world class racers as it is for the beginner skier.

If you are nervous or scared, you will be tense. Your balance will be affected because all of your muscles are tense — not only those used to hold your balance. Yet some people have this natural courage (insanity?). Teenage boys often are quite ready to go full speed without knowing where they are going. Speed without direction, in life or on the slopes, is not intelligent.

If you find that you're a bit apprehensive about a downhill run, start with the snow plow or use a half wedge with one ski in the track and the other wedging and slowing you. Once near the bottom of the slope put both skis in the track and ride it out. Work to go just a little faster each time. Start your parallel skiing just a bit higher on the hill and increase your confidence.

Bend forward and think of being aggressive. The typical beginner carries the weight back, as if digging in with the heels. This won't work. Bend the knees slightly, bend forward at the hips and hold your hands in front of you. This should get your weight forward and provide you with the aggressive feeling and control that you want.

Going Faster

To zoom down the hill, you have to reduce the air resistance against your body. The faster you go, the greater the air resistance. To decrease wind resistance and ski faster, get into a tuck position. Bend the knees 90 degrees or more. Bring your chest down to your thighs. Keep your weight forward. Tuck your poles under your arm pits. The angle at the elbow will be 90 degrees. So make yourself into an egg — and fly!

One of the world's top three skiers does not go all the way down to the "egg" position. He keeps his legs almost straight. The reason, he says, is that while the egg position is more effective, it tires his thigh muscles, and he must be ready to climb the next hill. He sacrifices some downhill speed so that he can rest for the uphill climb. His view is definitely in the minority, but it may be worth thinking about.

As a recreational skier, you can control where you ski and how fast you will take the hills. But racers have to take steep downhills, as steep as 40 degrees, at top speeds, and sometimes for several minutes. At the 1995 World Championships in Thunder Bay, Ontario, Canada, there was a downhill run of more than two minutes.

If you do Alpine skiing, your Alpine skills will help you on your downhill runs. In Norway, we often bring in the Alpine downhill coaches to assist our Nordic skiers in their downhill techniques. After all, skiing is skiing!

Skiing Different Types of Snow

Powder is the ultimate, but it may be unforgiving. If you are lucky enough to get powder on a hill, or if you have decided to go far off the beaten track, you can have the greatest experience of your life.

Keep your weight equally distributed when skiing downhill in powder. Make your turns as fast or as slow as you like, but finish every turn. If you head straight down the hill, you may be in a little trouble and may have to brake yourself with a "head plant" in the deep snow. So make your full turn to control your speed. The powder helps to slow you down, but it won't do it all.

If you haven't done it before, find a slight slope with new powder. Walk up the hill a little way, and then ski straight down. Put more weight on the left ski, then the right. See how your balance feels. You will find that even distribution is best. After a few straight runs to get the feel, try a straight run while you are bending your knees. Move your hips up and down.

Once you feel comfortable with your straight shots down the hill, you are ready to try a Telemark or a parallel turn. (See Chapter 6.) Plant your pole in the direction you want to turn. Telemarkers will move the opposite ski forward and the near ski back while they carve the turn. Parallel skiers will emphasize the weight on the outside ski but can edge both skis in making the turn.

Checklist

1) Bend forward with your weight slightly on your toes.
2) Get into a crouch position or an "egg" position if you want to go faster.
3) Keep your weight on both skis.
4) Be ready to absorb the bumps with your legs by keeping your knees bent.

6

Stopping
and Turning

Stopping and turning are related movements. The simplest type of stop and turn develops from the wedge position. You simply slide the skis out at the tails, edge the inside edges, and you will slow and stop. To turn, slide one ski out at the tail and edge it, turning in the direction it is pointing. If you are going too fast down a hill, you merely turn up the hill and you will stop.

Skills Needed

- Sliding a ski out and in.
- Edging on the inside of each ski.
- Steering the skis with the lower body.
- Stepping out with one ski while the weight is on the other one.

To *slide* the ski: Put your weight on one ski and slide the other out with the base of the ski flat on the snow.

You can practice this at home on a rug or wait until you are on the snow. It is just a matter of balance. First, slide one ski out, then bring the skis together. Then slide the other ski out and bring the skis together. When you can do this comfortably, slide into a half wedge position by moving just the tail of one ski outward, keeping the tips of the two skis together.

Once you are on the snow, repeat the drills. When you feel comfortable with the one-legged sliding, slide both tails outward and make a full wedge position. Do this several times. After you have mastered sliding to the wedge, simply wedge your skis and bring your knees together. This will edge the inside edges of your skis, and you will be in the stopping wedge posture, commonly called the "snow plow."

To *edge* the skis: Move the knee inward while keeping the ankle stiff. This pulls the outside of the ski up, and your inside edge is "edged" into the snow. You may use this technique when traversing across a hill if your skis begin to slip downhill. You will also use it in some turns. It is also essential in the wedge stop or snow plow.

To *steer* the skis: Turn the whole leg in the direction that you want the ski to go. This is actually done in the hips where the thigh bone is turned or "rotated" around its long axis. But the key is the connection of the foot to the ski. If the foot moves, the ski will move.

To *step*: Put all of your weight on one ski while you lift and move the other outward.

To *stop in a prepared trail*: Lift one ski out of the track and put it into a wedge position. You can lift the ski and put it in that position, or you can lift it out of the track, put it on the snow, then slide it to the wedge position. Once it is wedged, you angle your knee and ankle inward so that the ski "edges" then you put more weight on that ski to increase the edging effect and to push against the snow to slow or stop your momentum.

To *stop out of the trail while coming down a hill*: Slide both skis out with the toes in and the tails out. The wider the angle of tail to tip, the greater your potential stopping power. Once they are in the proper position, bring the knees and ankles inward to create edges. This edging pushes against the loose snow and slows you down.

Another way to stop if you are on an open hill is to turn up into the hill. Let the skis slide as you steer them toward the uphill direction, then edge the lower ski as you continue to steer away from the fall line (the line directly down the hill).

The Wedge

Find a slight incline, such as at the bottom of a hill. Climb up and slide down. Try it first with the skis flat on the snow. Move the tails in and out, getting

the feel of sliding into the wedge then back into the parallel position. Now move a little higher on the hill and start down. As you slide your skis out into the wedge, lower your hips and bring the knees and ankles inward for edging. If you don't stop, try a wider wedge position, with the heels farther out. Next try greater edging by bending the ankle and the knee even more.

The Wedge Turn

The wedge turn is generally used by beginners and by others when the snow is hard or packed. From the narrow wedge position with your skis sliding down the hill, steer both skis with your knees and feet.

To execute the wedge turn, simply steer both skis with your knees and feet as shown in the series of photographs above.

For a sharper turn, you can put more weight on the ski that you want to be the outside ski in your turn. Edge the ski by bringing the knee and ankle closer to the middle of the wedge as you lean outward on that ski. In other words, put your weight on the ski that is pointing in the direction that you want to go. So put your weight on the right ski if you want to turn left, or the left ski if you want to turn right. Keep your hands low and the tips of the poles pointed backward. And presto, you're there.

Then you can make one turn in the other direction. This is called "linking" turns. When you feel comfortable with this activity, move farther up the hill and link some more exaggerated turns. As your turns become sharper, you will probably notice that you are edging your outside ski a bit. That's OK.

The Step Turn

The step turn is more practical when the snow is soft, which is when the wedge turn is more difficult to use. It can, however, be used on harder snow, but it will not stop you as quickly as the wedge. It is an essential turn for all skiers, even the world class skiers use it often when they need a "sure-footed" turn.

While moving down the fall line, step out with the tip of the ski that you want to be the inside ski in your turn. The tip of the inside ski moves away from the tip of the other, but the tails stay close together. Once you have stepped with

The Step Turn is essential for all skiers.

the one ski, put your weight on it and bring the other ski, the outside ski, parallel. Keep your ankles and knees flexed during the turn. Repeat the same movements until you have turned as far as you want to turn. Then practice coming back the other way. As you do this, move your shoulders, arms and hands in the direction of the turn.

If one ski slips, take many small steps so that the skis do not separate too far and require too much of a weight shift. Keep your body partially crouched so that your hips are closer to your knees and ankles — which will be controlling your turn. As you become more advanced you can take bigger steps, but for now, keep it simple.

The step turn is accomplished in three easy steps — repeated if necessary to complete the turn.

1) Step in the direction that you want to turn. The tips of the skis must be farther apart than the tails. The ski with which you step becomes the inside of the turning arc.

2) Shift your weight quickly to the inside ski then bring the other ski up to it and parallel.

3) Repeat this action with as many quick steps as are needed to complete the turn. Beginners will take smaller steps than will more advanced skiers.

Intermediate Turns

The Skate Turn

Start on a hill that is not too challenging until you get the feel of the turn. The skate turn is similar to the step turn, but it is more dynamic. Instead of merely stepping out on one ski, you push off the other ski as you step. The push-off ski is edged, and the body is propelled forward, diagonally toward the stepped-out ski. (See photos below.) The force of the push off brings the body over the stepped ski so the next turn step can be quickly continued. A double poling action can aid in the force and quickness of this turn.

The Swing Turn

The swing turn is a combination of the wedge and the step turn. While traversing across the mountain:

1) Lift or slide the tail of the uphill ski. This forms a wedge.

2) Put your weight on the uphill ski.

3) At the completion of the turn, the tail of the inside ski is brought inward so that you are again skiing with the skis parallel. This can be done while flattening the skis on the snow and side slipping as the parallel position is regained.

The Stem Christie

A slightly advanced method of turning, yet quite similar to the basic turn, is the "stem christie." The stem christie (sometimes called the wedge christie) combines the wedge, edging and stepping to make a higher speed turn which is effective on harder snow. The "stem" is the movement of the uphill ski outward into a modified wedge. The "christie" is named for the town where the turn was first used and popularized — Christiania. Christiania was the former name for the modern city of Oslo.

While skiing down an incline steeper than that used for the wedge turn, plant the pole near the tip of the downhill ski — the ski which will be on the inside of your turn. Step out with the ski on the other side (the uphill ski), moving the tail farther out than the tip. (This is the stem.) Put your weight on this ski and edge it so that it becomes the dominant ski. You will begin to turn in the direction that it is facing. Bring the second ski parallel with the first. Repeat the same steps so that you are stepping further across the hill. Ride the turn on the outside ski. Then bring the inside ski parallel.

If you can put your weight the inside edge of the uphill ski after you have stemmed, the turn should complete itself. (Turns which use the edging of the outside ski are more effective if the ski has a side cut. This is discussed in the chapter on equipment.)

You can do this turn by making a series of stems. In a more advanced turn you would stem, put the weight on the outside ski, and ride it around until the turn is completed.

The Parallel Turn

Parallel turns are more advanced turns which are used for wider curves and generally at higher speeds. It is often preferable when the snow is consistent but perhaps a bit slippery. The parallel turn provides a better side-to-side balance for these conditions.

A parallel turn is like a stem christie, but without the stem. Instead of stemming the skis, you will slide them. The parallel turn starts with planting the pole about even with the inside ski tip. The pole plant will be just behind the tip of the ski. The plant of the pole takes the weight off the ski next to the pole, the inside ski of the turn, and makes it easier to slide. You will be turning around the pole.

While advanced skiers will execute the turn with the skis close together, the intermediate skier will probably find it easier to keep the skis about shoulder width apart. This aids in balance, but makes it a bit harder to turn.

If you have skied Alpine, you are used to shorter poles. Because the cross country pole is longer than an Alpine pole, you will plant the pole a bit more forward. The progression is as follows:

1) Bend downward by flexing the ankles and knees.

2) Plant the pole as you extend your legs. This puts more weight on the skis but as you reach the top of the extension there is less weight on the skis so they turn more easily. As you do this your torso should move upward and forward.

3) Steer the skis in the new direction using both the knees and feet to make the turn. Emphasize turning the inside ski so that you don't bring the outside ski too wide and make the turn into a stem christie.

4) Flex the ankles and knees again to edge the skis and put more weight on them.

5) If you are going to link parallel turns going down the hill, prepare immediately for the next turn. Bend the legs, plant the pole as you extend your legs, turn the skis, then bend the legs again.

The Telemark Turn

The Telemark turn is the oldest of the high-speed turns. It was developed in the area of Telemark, 100 miles southwest of Oslo. It is used extensively on the hills in the United States and in Norway today. One of its major advantages is that it is effective in heavy deep snow or when carrying a heavy backpack. It is also used by ski jumpers to control their speed after they have landed. (We'll save ski jumping for the next book!)

The Telemark turn is a steered turn. As opposed to the other turns so far discussed, the Telemark turn does not keep the tips near each other. The inside ski is dropped far back with its tip coming close to the boot of the forward ski but angled toward the other ski.

The Telemark turn starts, as does the wedge or stem turn, with the weight on the uphill ski — the turning ski. The pole is planted as in the other high-speed turns. The inside knee of the turn drops down within a few inches of the snow in sharp turns. This is what pushes the inside ski backwards. The weight will be fairly evenly distributed between your two feet.

The amount of weight shifted and the amount of knee flex depend on the snow conditions and the degree of arc desired. In softer snow or for a longer turning radius, there would be less weight on the turning ski. Conversely, on hard snow or for quicker turns, the weight shift will be more pronounced. Of course, a ski with a greater side cut will also aid in the turn.

The wide ski position is very stable in the forward-backward dimension, but is not stable in the right-left dimension. For this reason Telemark skiers often hold their arms outward for more balance. However, as they become more advanced, this is not necessary nor desirable.

While an Alpine skier would have the upper body facing down the hill, Telemark skiers face up the hill. For slow turns this is not so important, but for sharper turns it is critical.

To execute the turn:

1) With the torso angled just slightly forward, the outside ski (the left ski if turning right) is pushed forward.

2) As the ski is pressed forward, bend at the knee and put weight on the ski. The knee should be over the toes.

3) The inside ski slides backward and the tip points inward. (In sharp turns, the tip of the inside ski may come almost back to the boot of the outside ski.)

4) The sharper the turn, the greater the knee bend. In sharp turns, the angles at the knees may be close to 90 degrees.

5) Let your weight be primarily on your front ski. There need only be enough weight on the rear ski to control its direction. But for some turns, you will want both skis working for you. You will need to have the weight evenly distributed and the edge the turning sides of both skis — both right edges if you are turning right.

6) Steer the skis with your feet and knees to make the turn. Think of the big toe of your forward ski, and the little toe of your rear ski as steering your skis.

7) Your shoulders twist up hill; the sharper the turn, the more counter rotation of your shoulders up the hill.

In deep powder, you will weight both skis, as if you were skiing only one ski. If you are making a parallel turn, you will both weight and edge the two skis. In telemarking you will have a good deal of weight on the rear ski because it is acting as an extension of the front ski — like one long ski.

The Telemark turn is particularly useful when you need forward-backward stability. This is likely to be the case when you are skiing very deep powder, crusty snow or crud — that chopped up junky snow which we often encounter. These snow conditions may often slow your skis and throw your balance forward. The wider forward-backward base of the Telemark can reduce the problems.

Special Situations

The challenge of the steeps is that everything continually changes. Snow consistency (light or heavy), steepness, degree of friction (ice or powder), and snow composition (crud and crust) are some of the variations that you will experience. With so many variations, just one or two types of turns will not be enough for the skier who wants to challenge the mountain.

Jump turns often are the salvation for the advanced skier who is in difficult snow. These are parallel-like turns which can get you out of the difficult crud and allow you to turn in the air. Bend your knees and plant your pole, then jump from both feet. As your skis come up bend your knees even more so that you can get your skis farther from the snow. Once airborne, turn your skis in the direction you want to go, then land. Your pole plant will vary depending on the steepness of the slope. It can be as far back as your heel in steep terrain.

In very difficult snow this type of turn can be your greatest salvation. Make a series of jumps: jump turn right, then jump turn left. As you land after each turn and your knees sink down toward your skis, you will be ready for your next turn. If you are in deep crud, you may not want to link your turns, but rather traverse then make a 180-degree jump and come back the other way. It is a technique which requires practice — but when you need it you need it!

Drills

Wedge Stop

1) Slide your skis out bringing the tips close together and the tails apart. The greater the angle, the more potential stopping power.

2) Edge the inside edges of the skis by bringing the knees and ankles inward, while lowering your hips.

3) The greater the angle of the ski edges, the more potential stopping power.

4) To increase the stopping power steer the heel of your boot more outward (for wedge width) and the ankle more inward for greater edging. Feel the pressure on the inside of your big toe so that you have more inward pressure on the inside front edges of the skis.

Sliding the Ski

1) Keeping your ski tips in approximately the same spot, slide the tail of one ski out.

2) Then follow with the other ski so that they are parallel.

3) Continue this sliding drill until the ski tails have scribed a complete circle.

4) Then go back the other way until you have another completed circle.

Edging the Ski

1) While standing on both skis, move your knees and ankles to the right slowly.

2) Then move them to the left.

3) Check the skis to see that they are edging with the movement of your ankles.

In a wedge position:

1) Lower your hips and bring both knees and ankles inward.

2) Check to see that the outside edges of the skis are moving upward.

3) Now lean forward and feel the pressure on the inside edge of the big toe.

Steering the Ski

1) Slide one ski outward about 10 inches.

2) Slide the tip out, then in. Get the feeling that your foot is steering the ski.

3) Try it with the other ski.

Stepping with the Ski

1) Use the same drill as the sliding drill, but lift each ski and step with it until you have completed a circle. This is called a star turn if you are not moving. When moving it is the step turn.

7

Skating

For many years, the skate has been used by skiers as they passed others who were skiing in the same tracks. It was also commonly used in making turns. However, it has been used in races only for the past several years. As it became more popular for racers, recreational skiers began to use the technique more often. Now special wide trails are often prepared just for the skaters, while the classical skiers still ski in their two-track trails — if they are available.

Skating is at the same time a simple and an advanced method for cross country skiing. While on the one hand many people learn to skate much quicker than they learn the classic technique, ski racers universally will skate if it is allowed. In ski races, the skaters are 10 to 30 percent faster than the classical, diagonal stride skiers. For the same amount of exertion, a skater can go at least 10 percent faster. A study of the Italian National Ski team showed that for the same speed, the skating techniques used 15 to 30 percent less energy than the classical technique. For these reasons, as you advance in skiing you will probably want to develop an efficient skating technique.

Note Sindre's longer poles (4 to 6 inches – 10 to 15 centimeters) and shorter skis (4 to 6 inches) for skating compared with his shorter poles and longer skis for his classic diagonal stride skiing.

Marathon Skate

The skate is used for speed on level terrain, skiing a curve and climbing hills. Slightly different techniques are used for each — particularly in how and when the poles are planted. There are also variations in the angle of the skis, with less of an angle on the flat land but a greater angle on the steeper hills.

There are several types of skating:

1) One-sided skating or "the marathon skate" uses only one ski to push and the other to glide. You will double pole with each skating movement.

* Double pole and skate with right ski — glide -- repeat the skate, glide sequence

One ski in the track while skating on the other

2) Two-sided skating uses different poling methods. The Norwegians call these "dances" while the Americans and many others often label them by the "V" shape of the skis.

    a. The single dance (V1 skate) uses a double pole plant for every other skating move. So the pole plant would come on every right skate or on every left skate. (In the V1 there is only one double pole plant for a complete skating cycle of two skates — a right and a left.)

* Double pole and skate with right ski — glide on the left ski — skate with left ski — glide on the right ski

Single dance (Torgny Mogren, World Champion in 1993)

b. The double dance (V2 technique) uses a double pole plant on each skating move — left and right pushes. The pole plant precedes the push off of the skating ski.

* Double pole and skate with right ski — glide on the left ski — then double pole and skate with left ski — glide on the right ski

c. The paddle dance uses pole plants in which one pole is planted just an instant before the other. It is almost like a double pole plant but the plant of the poles is staggered by about .1 to .2 of a second. The arms look somewhat like a canoe paddler where the lower arm starts to apply power just before the upper arm begins to apply power. The poles are planted on every other skate as in the V1. If you were poling with the left leg skate, it would look like the photos on the following page.

Paddle dance

* *Poles (left, right) — skate left — glide on right ski — skate right ski — glide on left ski*

    d. The diagonal dance (diagonal V) is used for steeper uphill grades. It is like the herringbone, but the skate and pole action is so forceful that there is some glide on each ski. The poles are planted alternately with the right pole being planted as the left ski begins its skate, then the left pole is planted when the right ski begins its skate.

* *Right skate, left pole — short glide on left — left skate, right pole — short glide on right.*

General Principles of Skating

Body Position

The body should be nearly erect, with only a slight bend at the waist. The feet should be close together to aid in power and balance.

The Eye Focus

Focus the eyes in the direction of the gliding ski — about 10 yards ahead. The eyes are crucial to balance and are essential in evaluating the upcoming terrain.

The Force Phase

It is easier to practice the force phase initially without poles. In this way it is just about like roller or ice skating. The arms swing freely and the legs provide the power. Just as in walking or running, the left arm swings forward forcefully

1

2

3

4

as the left leg pushes back in the skating action. Then glide on the right leg for a short distance. Then push off from the right leg.

The angle of the skating ski will not be too wide as you learn to skate. It is enough that you get some edging for the backward force. As you do this, think of the hips, not the legs, as providing your power. Let the skis do the work as the big muscles of the hips force them backward.

The force phase in the skating technique will last longer than that in the classical technique. It may last well over half a second. An angle of about 30 degrees will give a sufficient force pad. Lean forward and twist your torso slightly toward the pushing ski. Leaning will edge the ski so that you can push off. As you generate more speed, the angle of the skis will be reduced. As you go up steeper hills, the angle will greatly increase.

In skating it is important to remember that you are trying to push the snow sideways. Push with the whole foot — not just the toes. In fact it feels like you are pushing with your heel.

The Glide

The glide requires balance. The center of gravity, which is in the middle of your hips when you are standing up, moves over the gliding ski. This phase lasts from the end of the force phase of the pushing ski to the beginning of the skating force from the gliding ski. The shoulders should be perpendicular to the gliding ski to keep the body correctly aligned.

A rule which we always use is that the nose, knee and gliding ski must all be in a vertical line. This allows you to move your center of gravity effectively to the gliding ski.

The Recovery Phase

After the skating ski is pushed back in the power phase and the glide is effected, the skating leg moves forward to become the gliding ski on the next stride. In order to make certain that the legs are close it is a good idea to practice having the boot of the skating ski touch the gliding ski boot on the recovery step.

Double Poling

You have already done double poling but there are a few different concerns to consider while poling during skating. The poling action starts with your body totally erect, even on the toes. The poles are planted about 6 to 12 inches (15 to 30 cm) behind the hands. This is approximately next to the toes of the boots. Your body weight on the poles begins the thrust. You bend at the waist forcefully to develop the initial thrust.

The angle of your torso on the poling movement should be between 45 and 60 degrees. Some racers will bend to 90 degrees at the start to develop maximum power. The elbow will now be flexed about 90 degrees. The final thrust is then performed by the muscles of the upper back and shoulders (latissimus dorsi and posterior deltoids) and the back of the upper arm (triceps). The triceps extend the arm fully in the final thrust. Your hands are close to your knees, maybe below your knees. The arms then move forward in the recovery phase with the pole tips staying close to the snow.

Some Variations of Skating

One-Side Skating (The Marathon Skate)

To use this technique, start with both skis parallel and both poles planted. It will be often used if you are skating in tracks. The weight is partially shifted to the ski which will push. The torso bends downward as the poling action begins and the skat-

Marathon Skating

ing ski is forced backward. At the end of the force phase the skating ski and the poles recover and the skier glides on the gliding ski. When the momentum begins to slow, the same process is repeated with the same skating ski.

So the sequence is as follows:

1) Poles are planted and the tip of the skating ski is lifted outward to about 30 degrees.

2) The torso bends forward at the waist and begins the push backward on the poles and the skating ski pushes backward.

3) The torso continues to bend (while the arms push the poles to the end of the thrust) and the skating ski finishes its force phase.

4) The skating ski and the arms recover to the original position and the glide continues on the gliding ski.

When skating a curve or skiing uphill, the cycle (from pole plant to pole plant) is increased — with more rapid kicking and poling. When skiing slightly downhill the cycle can be slowed.

The one-sided skate is reasonably fast and can be used in a narrower area than can the double-sided skating techniques. It is also quite fast when skiing a curve — with the inside ski used as the gliding ski. And in slight downhill runs it is fast, particularly if done in a tuck and without poling. However, it is not as effective as other skating techniques in going up a steeper incline, and if there is no track, the gliding ski is more difficult to control. In racing it is used only when the snow in the track is faster than the snow on the path.

Many ski areas have flat areas tailored to the skating skier. In other places you will probably ski in the tracks. To skate in the tracks, using the marathon skate, lift one leg out of the tracks and angle it so that the tip is farther away from the tracks than the tail is. You won't need to worry about getting the force ski out of the way of the gliding ski, because the gliding ski will be deeper since it is in the track. Take several skates with one ski while gliding on the other, then put the skating ski in the track and skate with the other ski.

Your longer poles should easily reach behind the angled ski. Plant both poles behind the ski and push off on the force ski. Your hips will be closer to the angled ski because you will be pushing hard for power. As soon as the power is developed bring the hips back over the gliding ski.

Single Dance (V1)

The V1 is a high-speed technique used on the flat and when there is a slope of few degrees. The snow should be fast (old snow). For many skaters the single dance technique is the fastest for the slight downhill path.

Poling in the single dance technique occurs every two or more strides. Every two is most common. Assuming that the skier will pole on every right skate, the poles will be planted with the arms outstretched and the poles angled backward so that the plant is near the toe binding. The plant must be close to the skis.

Single Dance (Torgeir Bjorn, Technique Coach for the Norwegian National Team)

The body bends forward applying the body weight to the poles as the right ski begins to skate. The angle of the skate will be less than 30 degrees. The angle will be greater if going uphill and will be less if the skier is moving fast, such as downhill. The reduced angle allows for a longer skating stride.

The gliding ski (left ski) will be angled slightly outward, not straight ahead as in the marathon skate. As the right leg finishes its kick, the skier glides until the momentum slows then kicks back with the left ski, which will have a slightly larger angle. The poles are recovered and made ready for the next pole plant. The timing is:

* Pole-skate – glide – skate – glide – pole-skate – glide – skate – glide

Good skaters can go 8 to 10 yards per single stride, even on a slight uphill, using this technique.

The Double Dance (V2)

This is probably the fastest skating technique if you are going slightly uphill, but it is difficult because it requires great balance and it can be more exhausting. One double poling occurs with the beginning of each skate when the legs are together. It is used primarily in uphill skiing which is a little steeper than that for which the V1 is used. Fast old snow is also a big plus if you are going to use this technique.

The poles are planted, as in all double poling, quite close to the toe binding of the boots. The body, which weights the poles, is similar to that of the single dance (V1). In high-speed skiing, the angle of the torso to the thighs may vary from 15 to nearly 90 degrees through the cycle.

The angle of the skating ski will vary with the speed and the frequency of skates — the number of skates per minute. The faster the frequency of the skating strides, the greater the angle of the skating ski. The longer the strides, the less the angle — somewhere around 15 degrees.

For most of the stride only one ski is on the snow. Then there is that period when both poles are in the air recovering, and you are riding only on the gliding ski — so good balance is essential.

Paddle Dance

The center of gravity (the center of the hips) must flow smoothly from one ski to the other without too much movement to the side or without excessive up and down movement. This is a major factor in making this technique the most difficult to learn effectively.

The Paddle Dance

The paddle dance is superior on steep uphill climbs when racing in competition. It is a difficult technique to master, but when learned it offers the skier more effective balance throughout the cycle — as opposed to the double dance which requires the better balance. The paddle dance can also be used on the flat when the snow is slower.

As said before, the technique gets its name from the fact that the arm action resembles that of a canoeist, with one arm starting downward before the other does. The poling is always timed with the ski on one side — as in the single dance

59

Paddle Dance (rear view, uphill)

(V1) technique. The ski which is timed with the first pole plant is called the "drive" ski. The other is called the "hang" ski. If there is a slope coming from one side, in addition to the slope you are climbing, the "hang" side ski will generally be on that uphill slope side.

The technique is as follows:

1) The drive ski begins its push with a slight angle (generally 12 to 15 degrees). The grip of the pole on that side is brought close to the midline of the body and planted quite far back with nearly a 30-degree angle backward to reach the toe of the near boot which has already begun its backward movement. The other ski, the "hang" ski, is being brought forward and is either just about to be set in the snow or has just hit the snow.

2) The second pole (the hang side pole) is quickly planted next to the heel of the near boot (the hang side boot). Its angle backward is only about 15 degrees because it is reaching for the ski which has just been planted uphill. The pole is pushed backward as the hang side ski takes a short glide and the body weight is shifted to the gliding ski. Both poles should be pushing in the direction of the glide of the hang ski.

3) The hang-side ski begins its skate with a sharper outward angle (20 to 30 degrees), and the poles are recovering, ready for the next plants. (The recovery should be low without an upward movement of the pole baskets.) The

glide on the drive ski will be 10 to 20 percent longer than that on the hang ski. The weight is shifted to the gliding ski in preparation for the next skate.

The steeper the uphill slope the greater the outward angle of the skis and the less glide will be experienced. Meanwhile, the forward steps taken in the uphill movement are very long — the longest of any skating technique. When used on steep uphills, the steps are quick, and there is little glide. When used on flatter areas or on faster snow, the glides will be much longer.

The Diagonal Dance (Diagonal V)

The diagonal dance is used often for uphill climbs. It is similar to the herringbone, but there is a gliding phase with each step, and the pole action is single — that is, it is like the classic diagonal skiing technique where the left arm poles while the right ski skates, then the right arm poles while the left ski skates. This technique is used for even steeper hill climbing than are the previously mentioned techniques. It is not used often in World Cup meets, because the skiers are so strong that they do well with the other techniques.

When used for hill climbing, the skis' angle are much greater than the shallow angles used for skating on the flats and on moderate downhills. The angle of the ski from the direction of motion can be more than 30 degrees and as much as 45 degrees.

Because the skating is forceful, the upper body will rotate somewhat with the shoulder on the poling side reaching toward the skating ski side. From this forward position, the pole is planted near the heel of the boot to give a better angle of drive from the arm push. The rotation of the upper body is greater than in other skating styles because of the single poling technique.

Because of the uphill climb, the torso may be inclined farther forward. While some skaters keep their bodies nearly erect, others will bend to near 60 degrees. On the other hand, when used on the flats or slight downhills, the skater may nearly tuck and may, or may not, pole.

The diagonal V is one of the better ways for beginners to learn to skate. Without poles it develops the basic skating pattern, and with poles the timing is similar to the classic technique — which the beginner has already learned. It is less strenuous than the paddle dance for uphill skiing. And without poling, it allows for normal body coordination which is used in walking and running. The major disadvantage would be for those who want to attain a higher speed because the side-to-side movement of the diagonal dance reduces the forward speed.

Common Errors in Skating

■ The center of gravity moves up and down. There should be little up and down movement, only forward and side-to-side movement. Each additional and unnecessary movement impedes balance.

- Keeping a stance too wide during the skate without bringing the feet together. An excessively wide base requires that the center of gravity be shifted too far on each stride. This makes it much more difficult to balance.

- "Sitting," which brings the center of gravity (the hips) over the heels, reduces the chance for an effective force phase in the skate. It is not only inefficient but it takes a great deal of energy to hold a sitting position.

- Planting the poles inside the angled ski can trip the skier.

- Kicking only with the toes or the balls of the feet instead of with the whole foot is also inefficient.

A Final Note on Skating

As mentioned earlier, even beginners can start with skating — and may find it easier than the classic diagonal stride technique. When you see good skiers skating, the ease and freedom of the movement, and the joy of that freedom, become apparent. In Norway all of the good young skiers skate whether or not they are in competition. As you watch them fly around the tracks at Holmenkollen or pass you on the trails of Nordmarka, you get the feeling that they are flying on skis. And when you begin to do it yourself, you'll enjoy that same exhilarating feeling!

8

The Mechanics of Skiing

There are a number of mechanical factors which you may want to understand relating to skiing. You need to consider friction between your skis and the snow, forces generated by your arms and legs, what happens when you turn, and many other variables relative to the science of skiing. You may want to increase your understanding of these to ski more effectively. If you are not so interested in the "whys" and "wherefores" of skiing and are only interested in the "how to's," you can skip this chapter.

As you get more proficient at skiing technique, you will want to become more efficient. Elements, such as reducing drag by being in a more aerodynamic position or by having a better glide with your skis, are important. On the other hand, having the necessary friction under the power ski and having the leg and arm strength to maximize the push are also important. Let us look at a few of the components of the laws of physics and kinesiology that you will want to consider as you begin to increase your skiing ability.

Factors Affecting Balance

Gravity

Gravity is the pull of the earth on the skier. In simple terms, it is what you weigh. If you were skiing in outer space, you would be nearly weightless. But since most of your skiing will be on the planet Earth, you will be pulled toward the center of our world.

If it weren't for gravity, there would be no reason to learn technique. Without gravity one stride would develop a glide which would never stop. Such efficiency might be enjoyable for a while, but it would do nothing for your physical

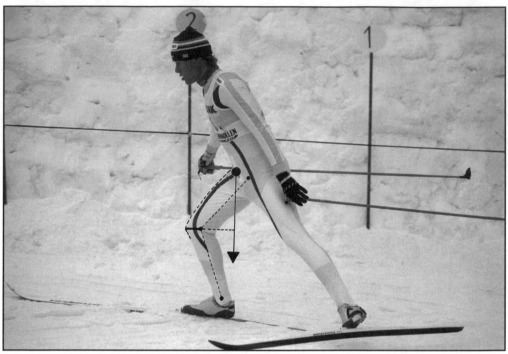

Center of Gravity

fitness and would soon be quite boring! Of course, gravity lessens when you go downhill and increases when you go uphill.

Gravity is also slightly affected by latitude — the closer you are to the equator the less there is. It is 0.005 less at the equator than the North Pole. So a skier in Oslo, Norway, would have to work about 0.4 percent harder to achieve the same speed as a skier in Quito, Ecuador. Additionally, there are factors of wind and snow friction (drag) which can aid a skier in Norway going downhill. The skier in Oslo would go about 0.2 percent faster downhill than the skier in Quito. On the other hand, the lesser gravity in Quito would make the equipment weigh 0.4 percent less, so climbing a hill would be easier near the equator. You can probably balance these two factors if you do your cross country skiing in Florida or the Caribbean!

Yet while the effect of gravity is actually the major factor related to ski speed, there are other ingredients.

Balance and Your Center of Gravity

The longer the ski stride and glide, the better your balance must be. Balance is achieved when the center of gravity of the body is exactly over the supporting foot or feet.

The center of gravity is where the exact center of the body's weight is concentrated. The pull of the earth's gravitational forces is centered in this part of your body. If you were to stick an imaginary needle through the middle of the body and the body were perfectly balanced, it would spin effortlessly around that point. You would have pierced the center of gravity.

If you were to balance a baseball bat on your finger, you will find that your finger will be farther away from the grip of the bat because there is less wood (weight) there. In fact, your finger may be two-thirds of the way toward the wide end of the bat. When you have balanced the bat, the center of gravity of the bat will be directly over your finger.

If you are standing erect, your center of gravity will generally be in the area of your hips. Most women have a center of gravity a bit lower than do men. A person with thin legs, but a heavy upper body would have a center of gravity higher than a person with a light upper body and heavy legs. If you bend forward with a 90-degree angle at your hips, your center of gravity will be outside your body and in front of the hips.

Balance and Your Base of Support

Your base is the foot, or feet, on which your weight is supported. In skiing down the fall line, it is equally balanced on both feet. If you are in a glide, it is totally on the gliding foot. If your center of gravity is not directly over the exact middle of your base, you will fall. If it goes too far past your base, you fall outward. If it doesn't go far enough, you fall inward. If it is too far back, you fall backward. And if it is too far forward, you fall forward. But because your feet are longer than they are wide, you have much less of a chance of falling forward or backward than you do to your side.

If you stand on one foot and do not fall, it means that your center of gravity is exactly over the base of support of your foot. However if you are walking, you don't shift your center of gravity totally over the supporting foot. It never quite gets there. Before you fall your other foot hits the ground, and you regain your balance. You are also aided by the muscles contracting on the outside of the supporting leg. They prevent your body from collapsing inward and falling away from the supporting leg.

The key to balance is being able to smoothly get your center of gravity exactly over the middle of your support base. The longer the glide, the more important this is. If you are taking short choppy steps up a hill in a herringbone series of strides, your center of gravity does not have to be transferred to the exact center of the base. This is because before you fall you have regained your balance by putting your weight on the other leg — just like in walking. But if the hill is steep, you will want all of your center of gravity on the pushing ski so that you can get the maximum amount of push on the snow.

If you were making quick turns while coming down a hill, you would lean into one turn, then quickly lean the other way as you make a turn in the other direction. Your center of gravity would not move out to the outside ski. Before you fell inward, you would make another turn which would catch your balance. If you have watched Alpine skiers, you would notice that the slalom skier, who makes very quick turns, always has his or her center of gravity inside of the feet.

But the downhill skier, who makes few turns, will be pretty well balanced on both legs most of the time.

During a series of quick turns, the centrifugal force of the turn pulls your body outward. If it gets as far as your outside ski, you would fall outward. So when turning, your center of gravity will not get quite out over the outside ski. It's just like riding a bicycle around a corner, you lean into the turn or you fall outward. But if you leaned when going straight, you would fall inward. So where you hold your center of gravity in order to keep your balance depends on whether you are going straight or turning and how high your center of gravity is over your skis.

In skiing you need to be able to develop the coordination which allows you to shift your center of gravity as far toward the supporting leg as is necessary for the length of your stride. The longer stride and glide require a more complete shift of the center of gravity over the supporting foot. And certainly you must be able to control the lateral movement of the center of gravity so that it never gets outside of your base or — down you go!

Negative Factors Affecting Speed

Friction

When gliding you want as little friction as possible. When generating force in the push-off ski, you want a great deal of friction. (For you engineers and physicists — a well-waxed ski has a coefficient of friction of about 0.05; the power ski in classical skiing must have a coefficient of at least 0.2 in the middle section of the ski when power is applied, and in skating, where the ski edge is dug into the snow, the value can come close to 1.0.)

What this means in practice is that, if you are skiing the classical diagonal technique, you must know how much of your ski is coming in contact with the snow when you push off. That part of the base of your ski must have a wax or a texture (waxless skis) which will give maximum friction. Then, when you glide you want that high friction wax to be off of the snow so that it does not create a hydrodynamic drag. And if you are skating, you can use a glide wax over your whole ski so that friction can be reduced when you glide.

Newer snow creates more drag than does older snow. The older snow has often undergone thawing and refreezing, or if it is in a track, has been compressed many times. The millions of individual flakes in new fallen snow, with each flake having six points, create more drag by having more "sharp" points in contact with the gliding ski. The individual flakes of the snow are compressed into larger crystals with fewer points to produce friction on the ski bottoms. And, of course, ice has even fewer contact points so glide is greatly enhanced by ice.

But the same characteristics of ice make it much more difficult to overcome the lack of friction (between the ice and the ski) with the pushing ski. The wax of the classical skier and the edge of the skater get far less grip on ice.

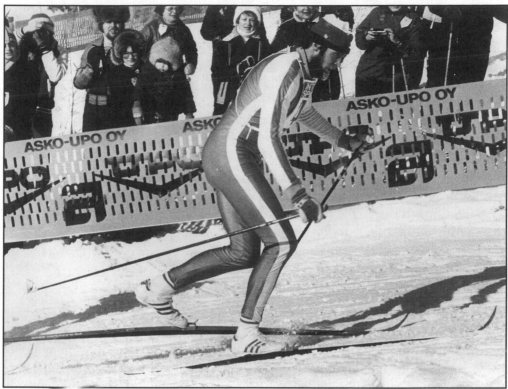

At 6 feet, 10 inches, Juha Mieto has plenty of aerodynamic drag, but his beard cost him the world championship by 0.01 seconds.

Drag

Drag is what slows you down. There are two kinds of drag. Hydrodynamic drag is the friction developed as the ski glides over the snow, along with the friction created by the thin layer of water which forms as the ski melts the snow under it.

Hydrodynamic drag is the result of increased friction between the ski and the thin coating of water under the ski. That water can become much thicker when skiing in warmer temperatures, such as occurs in the spring. And the thicker water can create a "suction" effect which greatly slows down the ski. Ski manufacturers have worked to develop structures for the bases for the skis which break up this suction effect.

Aerodynamic drag is the resistance of the air and wind against your body. When your speed doubles, your drag factor increases by 400 percent. A wind from the front increases aerodynamic drag while a wind from back reduces it. The more surface area your body uses to push against the air, the more drag you produce. Obviously that is why a tuck position when going downhill reduces drag. In fact, the tuck reduces wind resistance by more than 50 percent. (And that approximate 55 percent reduction in aerodynamic drag is multiplied by the square of the speed, so the faster you go the more important it is to be in an aerodynamic position.)

Clothing can reduce drag. Runners and cyclists have found that certain clothing can reduce drag by up to 10 percent. Tighter fitting clothing and a drag reducing hood can be obvious drag reducing aids. You have certainly seen the Olympic ice skaters wearing very tight body suits and head hoods. Ski racers have adopted the full body suits, but do not always use the drag reducing hoods.

The Total Energy Consumption

The energy consumption negative factors have been calculated by Dr. Erik Spring, professor of applied physics at the University of Helsinki in Finland. He is the scientific advisor to the Finnish world class skiers. His research indicates that the energy output of a skier is approximately:

- 30 percent to overcome the friction of the snow.
- 15 percent to overcome drag.
- 10 percent to move the skis forward after each power step.
- 5 percent to move the poles forward.

Decreasing the amount of friction by 10 percent reduces the output of energy by three percent. Similarly, a decrease in the energy consumption in any of these areas results in greater speed and efficiency. Better wax and more efficient waxing techniques are the major concerns here. But lighter skis and poles will also have an effect. So will more drag resistant clothes and a body position which will reduce drag.

In the 1980 Olympics, one of Finland's best skiers lost a race by 1/100th of a second. His long hair and beard had created more than enough drag to make that difference. In fact they were probably responsible for several yards difference in his race.

Overcoming Friction and Drag Resistance

Force

Force is the power generated which overcomes the friction of the snow and the drag of the air. Force is generated by the transfer of muscle power to the poles and the skis.

It is not only the amount of force and the angle of force which is important, but also the length of time that the force is applied to the snow. So, while a pole plant at a great angle backward would be more efficient in transferring muscle power to overcome the snow's friction, a longer poling action will apply that force longer.

Through the Poles

Obviously the amount of force you can exert backward is the amount of force you will generate forward. We all remember Newton's third law of motion

Full torso flexion and complete extension of the arms results in a longer poling action finishing with the poles nearly parallel to the snow for maximum force.

every action has an equal and opposite reaction. If you pushed on a pole which was perfectly vertical, you would have a resultant force which would be straight up. If you are using your poles to assist with a turn, your skis would be easier to slide around the turn (side slip). Use such a pole plant in a parallel turn or a stem christie.

Of course, most of the force which you want exerted through the poles is horizontal force — force directly horizontal and parallel with the snow. In order to have such a force, you would have to have a strong vertical wall to push against with your poles parallel to the snow. Naturally, this can never happen on the snow. None of our poling during skiing will ever be exactly vertical or horizontal. The closer your hands are to the snow, the more horizontal force is exerted because the poles are more horizontal. Consequently, as the poling stroke nears its finish, when your torso is bent lower and your hands are lower, the greater the potential of force that can be transferred through the poles. A skier will therefore never put the poles in the snow in a vertical plant. So when the objective is to move forward efficiently, the pole tips should always be behind your wrists.

Because there are two factors which affect the force transmitted through the poles (the angle of the pole plant and a longer poling action), the efficient skier must find the happy medium. If the objective is to move forward, the pole must always be planted at some angle backward.

The longer poles of the skater were designed to allow for a pole plant behind the ski which is farther away from the body. But the effect has been to give the skater a more efficient transmission of power through a pole which is set at a sharper angle to the snow than the shorter poles of the classical skier. So the skater can have just as long a poling action as the classical skier yet have the poles at a more effective angle to transmit that force throughout the arm stroke. But in addition to the more effective pole angle, the skater can actually take a longer poling stroke and apply force over a longer period of time.

If the pole plant moves the snow backward and therefore slips in the snow, the amount of potential force is reduced because friction (the "sticking" factor) is reduced. If one is poling on ice and the pole does not penetrate, there is likewise less friction so less force is exerted against the snow.

Another crucial factor in the application of force through the poles is the strength of the muscles of the upper back and the back of the upper arm, the latissimus dorsi and the triceps. Developing strength (the amount of force which can be developed in one contraction of a muscle) and muscular endurance (the number of repetitions the muscle group can accomplish without tiring) are both essential. Exercises for these muscle groups are discussed in Chapter 11.

The Swedish professor Bengt Saltin, in his keynote address at the International Congress on Skiing and Science in Arlberg, Austria, in 1996, said that the amount of energy expended on the arms or legs is about equal to the power and speed output. So don't underestimate the force potential of your poling action.

A Classical Skier's Show of Force

The classical skier's force is directly backward, and the glide directly forward. Such movements should be ideal. The problem is that the force ski or kicking ski will tend to slip backward a bit; this reduces the push, and the gliding ski may be slowed if the grip wax touches the snow and increases friction.

A Skating Skier's Show of Force

The skating skier gets a better grip on the snow by angling the ski outward. The farther out it is angled, the less distance through which force can be applied and the greater the angle in the opposite direction that the gliding ski must take. Because of the greater separation of the skis during the skating movements, the center of gravity must move farther laterally than it does in classical skiing. This may create a balance problem, particularly if the glide is long.

Lift

When you are coming downhill in a tuck position, with the back rounded, you can get a slight lift from the air moving quickly over the back. This is the same principle which is used in airplane wings and which lifts the plane (the Bernoulli Principle). Bicycle racers work very hard at getting an aerodynamic position with lift. An effective position can increase efficiency 10 to 20 percent. For the skier, the lift will reduce the friction of the snow.

Energy Expenditure

Body Mass

The weight of your body and your ski equipment is important for a couple of reasons. The more your leg, boot and ski weigh, the more energy you must exert to move that leg forward. When striding forward, your leg goes about twice as fast as your torso. Then, as you push off with the leg, your foot is nearly stationary. So you must drive the leg forward then have it stop. This is a major factor in energy expenditure and in fatigue. Using the skating technique is less costly in terms of these energy expenditure factors, which is another reason for skating being faster.

When you must lift a leg, such as when climbing hills, there is a greatly increased effect of fatigue. In addition to these forward (horizontal) movements, there is an energy cost in any rotational movement which the body performs.

While this would appear to favor the smaller skier, this is not the case. Larger skiers, because of greater muscle power, seem to be able to generate more power in nearly all areas of skiing, except when skiing uphill. The primary concern is whether the skier can generate more power than the resistances (air and snow) give friction.

Since it requires more force to move a greater body weight forward, your body weight does have a negative component. Also, the more you bend at the waist, the more energy that is expended to energize your back muscles which must hold up your torso. But the bent position reduces air drag. So if you are not going too fast, your body can be more erect to save the energy expenditure in your back muscles and to reduce fatigue.

The more erect position can also be used when going uphill, because the wind resistance is not very great. In addition, by being erect the center of gravity remains more effectively over the driving ski than it would be if the skier were bent forward. This should increase the ski's ability to develop maximum friction and a more effective push off.

A heavier skier also uses more energy when in a tuck position, because the muscles of the back and thighs need to support more weight. But the effect of gravity in generating more downhill speed may more than compensate for that energy expenditure. Also, because the heavier skier will undoubtedly have a greater cross sectional area creating wind resistance and drag, the tuck position should be more valuable in reducing those drag effects.

Increasing the Efficiency of Movement

To reduce the energy expended, the efficient skier will reduce the amount of weight lifted — body weight, ski and boot weight, and pole weight.

It is impossible to eliminate all up and down movement, but keep it to a minimum.

If the body's center of gravity is raised and lowered often, each time it is raised muscular energy must be expended by the leg and hip muscles. So the skier must determine whether the up-down movement, such as is used in double poling, increases the speed sufficiently to make up for the increased energy expenditure.

Side-to-side movement of the center of gravity, which is much greater in skaters than in classical skiers, also increases energy expenditures. As the center of gravity is moved to the gliding ski, muscular energy is used to both move it and to stop it. However, the other positive forces in skating somewhat compensate for this problem.

Excessive weight shift of hips and shoulders

Sufficient weight shift to get the head and center of gravity over the gliding skis

To keep your movements efficient, the skis should be kept close to the snow so that energy is not wasted in lifting them excessively. Beginning classical skiers often lift the skis, rather than slide them when moving them forward. Skaters, in recovering their skis from the push off to the glide phase, may lift the ski higher than it needs to be to clear the snow.

The pole baskets should also be kept close to the snow in recovery. For every inch or centimeter they are lifted, additional energy is used.

Increasing the Efficiency of the Body

The more force the legs and arms can generate in pushing the body forward, the faster you can go. Muscular strength in certain muscle groups is required for

Lifting the skis excessively during recovery uses extra energy.

Even champion skiers may bring their poles too high, resulting in an increase in energy expenditure.

this. Continuing this pushing action over thousands of repetitions requires both muscular endurance (endurance within the appropriate muscles) and cardiopulmonary endurance (endurance related to the heart and the oxygen-carrying capacity of the blood). Both of these will be discussed more fully in Chapter 11 as well.

Getting Even More Technical!

If you want to measure yourself against the best in the world, an analysis of World Cup racers was presented by Professor Ansgar Schwirtz of the Institute of Sports and Science at the International Congress on Skiing and Science in 1996. The accompanying chart summarizes his findings:

■ The speed (cycle velocity) was 7.1 meters per second for men and 6.0 for women.

■ The cycle time (full two skate sequence) 1.117 seconds for men and 1.09 for women.

You can figure out the rest from the figures. Basically, the men are stronger and travel faster, but the women increase their speed of strides (cycle time) to attempt to compensate.

So if you are a man and travel at seven meters per second or a woman travelling at six meters per second, join the World Cup racers.

More efficient poling action with the baskets close to the snow

Comparison of men and women in stride, frequency, etc.

Parameter	unit	male (n=14)		female (n=19)	
		X	s	X	s
cycle velocity	[m/s]	7.1	0.3	6.0**	0.3
cycle time	[s]	1.17	0.08	1.09**	0.05
cycle rate	[1/min]	51.3	3.4	55.4**	2.4
Ski-phases					
-thrust time	[s]	0.48	0.07	0.43*	0.05
-gliding time	[s]	0.69	0.06	0.65*	0.05
-thurst/cycle time	[%]	40.7	4.6	39.1	5.3
-gliding/cycle time	[%]	59.3	4.6	60.8	4.3
pole-phases					
-pole left	[s]	0.27	0.03	0.31**	0.03
-pole left/cycle time	[%]	23.3	2.6	28.7**	1.9
-pole left/thrust ski	[%]	56.3	7.0	72.1**	9.2
-pole right	[s]	0.28	0.04	0.32**	0.03
-pole right/cycle time	[%]	23.4	3.5	29.4**	2.2
-pole right/thrust ski	[%]	58.3	9.6	74.4**	10.4

* significant difference to the mean value male, $p<.05$

** significant difference to the mean value male, $p<.01$

9

Equipment

The earliest known ski was used 4,500 years ago. It was a bit over four feet long and five inches wide. Other skis were more than six feet long (two meters) and weighed six pounds (2.7 kg) per pair. Until about 100 years ago, skis were made of a single piece of birch, pine, hickory or other available wood. As skiing became more popular, the wooden wheel makers also made skis.

Ancient stone carving depicting the use of skis around 2000 B.C.

In the late 1800s, ski manufacturing factories were developed and soon laminated wood skis appeared. These were lighter than the solid wood skis. By the 1970s, synthetic materials found their place. Each development has allowed the skier to ski better on stronger, better shaped and technically superior equipment. And you are the beneficiary of this progress.

In 1974 the first fiberglass ski with a polyethylene base became the first of the synthetic skis. Now, with combinations of carbon fibers, Kevlar, fiberglass, acrylic foam and other modern materials, strong, lightweight skis are the order of the day. Today's skis weigh only a third of what the older solid wood skis weighed.

With the additional reduction of the weight of boots and bindings, skiers today achieve nearly a 15 percent energy savings when skiing the same speed as a skier of 50 years ago.

The Characteristics of the Ski

The shovel is the turned up front end of the ski. The shovel height indicates how high the shovel tip is from the main part of the ski. The tail is the rear end of the ski.

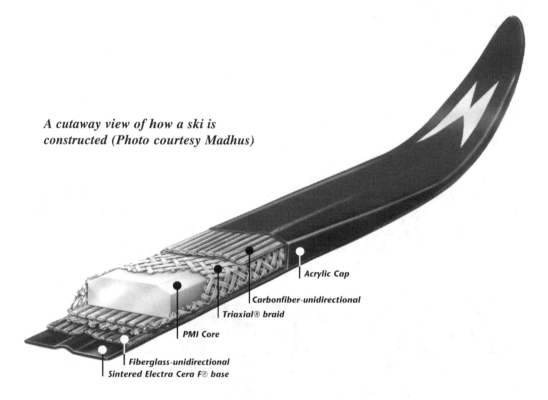

A cutaway view of how a ski is constructed (Photo courtesy Madhus)

Acrylic Cap

Carbonfiber-unidirectional

Triaxial® braid

PMI Core

Fiberglass-unidirectional

Sintered Electra Cera F® base

The side cut, or side camber, is the inward curve of the side of the ski from the shovel to the tip. The deeper this cut the greater the ability to turn. The bottom camber is the arch upward from the bottom of the tip to the bottom of the tail.

Length

The length of the skis is important. Until quite recently some skis were as long as 12 feet (3.5 meters). Some prehistoric skis had a long and a short ski so that the skier could push off on the short ski then glide on the long ski. Today, we use shorter skis for skating, because they are easier to push off with and longer skis for better glide in classical skiing. The skating skis will be about 4 to 6 inches (10 to 15 cm) shorter than the classic skis.

A longer ski is more stable when moving forward, gives a greater floating effect — with less weight per square inch on the snow — and would be faster in straight ahead gliding. However, it is less maneuverable and more difficult to turn than shorter skis.

Width

The body of the skis, which had been as wide as 5 inches (12 cm) to allow it to float on the powder, has been reduced to 1¾ to 2½ inches (4.5 to 6 cm) as machine-packed trails have become common. A wider ski is more stable, but is more difficult to control when traversing a slope. Measured at the waist (the middle of the ski); racing skis are about 1¾ inches (44-45 mm) wide; touring skis vary from 1¾ to 2¼ inches (45 to 55 mm); and downhill skis such as Telemark are about 2¼ inches (55 mm) to slightly wider.

Edges

The edges can be the same material as the base or can be metal. The metal edges grip better for more control, but add weight to the ski which will make it a bit slower. Where turning is important the metal is preferable, but if you are just skiing in prepared tracks you are generally better to opt for the lighter skis.

Shape

The shape of the ski allows for better turning. While competition skis have nearly parallel sides with the width of the ski decreasing slightly towards the front and back, recreational skis may have a reduced width in the middle allowing for better turning (a ski with a wider front and back).

Bottom Camber

The bottom camber (or arch) is evident when the ski is lying flat on the ground. Only a small part of the tip and tail should be touching the ground.

Stiffness

The stiffness of the ski is important because, if it bends too easily when you put weight on it, the sticky kicking area of the ski (the wax pocket) will touch the snow and will limit your glide. If it does not bend enough when you have nearly all of your weight on it, your kicking area will not make contact with the snow so you will not be able to generate power.

Side Cut

The side cut (waisting) allows for easier turning. The deeper the arc from the tip to the tail, with the middle being the narrowest, the quicker the ski can turn. The side cut for Alpine slalom skis is very great, because they are required to turn quickly. With Alpine racing skis, such as those used in Olympic racing, there is little or no side cut. This is also true for the Nordic cross country skis.

The side cut helps in turning, because when the full weight of the person is put on the inside edge of one ski, the arc of the side cut makes the ski follow that arc and turn. So if you put your weight on the inside edge of the right ski, the ski would turn toward the left. The greater the degree of arc, the tighter the ski will turn.

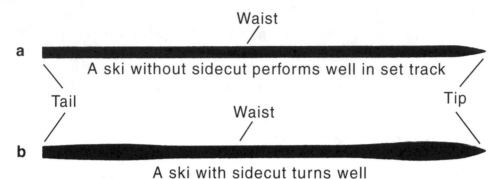

Waist

a

A ski without sidecut performs well in set track

Tail

Waist

Tip

b

A ski with sidecut turns well

Buying Skis

First determine the type of ski that you want. Mountain or Telemark skis are wider and have metal edges. They are therefore more stable and easier to turn, but they are heavier. The narrow trail skis are lighter but not quite as stable or responsive. If you are going to do all of your skiing on the mountain then the mountain skis are more appropriate.

Racing skis are quite narrow and require good balance. They are very light and very fast — if you can ski them. Touring skis are about halfway between the mountain and the racing skis. Neither of these has metal edges. There are also other types of skis.

If you skate, you may consider skis made especially for skating with reinforced sides to reduce the wear from the continued pushoffs of the skater. Beginners may want to stay with a wider ski for balance, but advanced skaters will opt for the racing type skis. Skaters will also usually use shorter skis.

Waxable or waxless is the next question. The beginner or the occasional skier may choose the waxless skis. But the true lover of the sport will choose the traditional waxable skis. The traditional skis have flat bottoms while the waxless skis will have a textured bottom in the middle of the base which allows the ski to slide forward and also dig into the snow on the kicking phase. Serious skiers will generally have several pairs of skis, including at least one pair of the waxless kind.

The **waxless skis** are occasionally used by top skiers when they know the conditions will change and they don't want to keep changing waxes. They have even been used in the Olympics when such conditions exist. They are also preferred by people who don't ski often and those who want maintenance free skis. Generally, these skis will drag a bit on the snow, because of the increased friction and they will not glide as well. Although they are "waxless," better performance can be gained by using a spray or a special wax to improve the glide.

Waxable skis are for those who want performance. With proper wax, they will glide better and give better traction in the kick phase. Because the snow can vary in many ways (wetness, temperature, icy conditions), the proper wax will give you better performance.

Next determine the length of ski you want. Longer skis will give you more float and glide and will be faster, but they are more difficult to maneuver. If you plan to skate, you will want shorter skis. For classical skiing, the most common method of determining length is to stand with your arm stretched upward. With the tail of the ski on the ground, the tip should come somewhere between your wrist and your palm. Lighter people can use shorter skis if they wish. Skating skis are usually about 4 to 6 inches (10 to 15 cm) shorter than the touring ski.

Fischer has now developed a shorter but wider ski which has the same "floating" and gliding abilities of the traditional skis. (Other manufacturers will probably soon follow.) These skis are easier to maneuver than the longer skis. They are particularly good for skating.

Find the ski with the proper stiffness (or flex). Have the ski shop expert pick a ski that is probably right for you. Factories make different flexes for each length of ski. Next, stand on a hard smooth surface. When you have your weight equally on both skis a sheet of paper should easily pass under the kicking area (wax pocket) of the ski. About 30 inches (75 cm) of ski should be off the ground.

When all of the weight is on one ski, the paper shouldn't be able to move. If your weight does not flatten the ski on to the snow (eliminating the bottom camber), your wax will not touch the snow and you will not be able to push forward with your power stride or when climbing. This will result in slipping and loss of power. In addition to being inefficient and frustrating, it is very tiring.

If the flex is too soft, your kicking wax will be on the snow when you are trying to glide and you will be slowed. Too soft a flex will also wear out the wax sooner. If you are more advanced and have a powerful kick, you will want a ski with a "harder flex" (more stiffness). However, less experienced skiers can generally use a softer flexed ski.

World and Olympic champion, Bjorn Daehlig of Norway, uses extremely stiff skis when he is in classic races. His kick is so powerful that he can straighten the ski and get the wax pocket on to the snow, then the ski will pop back and he is certain that he won't get any drag from the kick wax in the center of the ski. Manufacturers usually categorize their skis according to ideal weight capabilities. But do your own checking. Also, if you plan to do ski touring with a backpack remember to include the weight of the pack in your calculations.

Effective side cut is your next concern. For general use you will want a ski with some side cut (side camber). But if you are skiing only on prepared trails or you are in competition, you may want little or no side cut.

Make your final check. Once you have selected the skis which will best suit your needs, give one last check. With the ski bases together, put the tips on the floor. While holding the tail area, look along the ski to make certain that the side cuts are uniform and that the amount of flex in each ski matches. Also check to see that the bases are flat. A concave base will not ski well.

Next, with both hands grip the skis and push the bases together. Do the bases touch all along? If not, one may have a greater flex than the other. If a person can squeeze the bases together when gripping them in the middle with both hands, the flex is not too great. If they squeeze easily, the flex is probably too weak. (If you can squeeze them together with one hand they are definitely too weak.)

Boots

The original boots were the walking boots that the people of the cold North had to use to keep their feet from freezing off. As shoemaking developed, regular leather boots were used. Then, as special bindings were developed, special boots were needed to attach to the bindings. We still use leather boots, but they are much lighter, using plastic for the bottoms.

Alpina skating boot

Salomon boot and binding
for both classic and skating techniques

Normal recreational touring boots are leather high-tops with various combinations of plastic, rubber or combination bottoms. The better boots are double-laced with padded tops. Some recreational boots are lined. This has some advantages relative to warmth, but they are slower to dry. The same effect can be gained from thick woolen socks.

Other types of boots are available for "non-normal" situations. For spring skiing, when the snow is more watery, a rubberized boot may be preferable, because it can keep your feet dry. For racing, a low-cut lightweight boot is the answer. For mountain skiing, other specially made boots are available — usually a cross between a downhill boot and a touring boot.

Whatever the type of boot you need, insure a proper fit. There must be adequate room for the toes, which should not be pushed against the front of the boot. The sole should be rigid enough to keep the foot directly over the ski. It should be snug enough to reduce lateral movement.

Choose the type of boot you want before you choose the binding, because most manufacturers build a boot and binding combination. One company's boot won't always fit another company's binding.

Bindings

The earliest bindings were leather thongs or pieces of twine which bound the ski to the walking boots of the early Scandinavians. As steel came into use, toe pieces were fashioned which gave the skier greater control over the ski. Now steel, aluminum or plastic gives us more control as well as greater ease in getting into and out of our bindings.

Rottefella binding

Today, bindings are somewhat standardized with a toe clip which holds the toe of the boot firm to the ski but allows the heel to lift. This allows the skier to take long strides and to move more easily uphill. But since the boot can still come fully in contact with the ski, on downhill runs the whole foot can be used for steering. To make this easier, a foot plate is part of the binding. The boot, when flat on the ski, fits into ridges on the foot plate.

Fischer boot showing toe clip

Some companies make bindings and foot plates which require their shoes for proper fit. One will have a raised area running the length of the plate and will require a shoe with an identically matched groove in the sole and heel of the boot in order to work correctly. Another will have two ridges which will fit into two grooves in the sole and heel. So be certain that your boots match your bindings. For instance, Salomon makes both the boot and the binding, as well as the ski; Rottefella does not make boots so you would buy a boot such as an Alpina to match the bindings.

Bindings formerly used only for racing are now the standard for all. You step into the binding, clamp it, and you are ready to

Alpina boot with Rottefella binding   **Alfa boot with Rottefella binding**

ski. Because of the close tolerances of the bindings, a little snow in the gripping section can make it inoperable. So if you are standing in the snow and your bindings don't click shut easily, clean the binding bar on the front of the boot and brush out or blow out any snow in the binding.

While Alpine skis have releases to allow the boot to come out of the binding in a fall, Nordic bindings generally do not. The exceptions are special Alpine-type bindings for some mountain or Telemark skis which will release in a fall.

Poles

As far as we know the original prehistoric skiers did not use poles. It wasn't until about 1500 A.D. that we find evidence of a pole being used. It apparently was used to push, stop and turn. Solid wooden poles appeared about 100 years ago, but gave way to the lighter bamboo poles. Now these have been replaced by very light synthetics — first fiberglass, now carbon or Kevlar.

Since about half of the force of propulsion comes from the upper body, the poles are extremely important. They must be strong, light and of a proper length to transmit as much horizontal force as possible. In decreasing order of strength for weight we have: Kevlar, carbon, fiberglass and other synthetics. The stiffer the pole, the more energy is transferred to the snow with the resulting forward force.

The baskets, the devices on the bottom of the poles, stop the pole tip from going deeper into the snow. Through more modern design they are also becoming lighter, but because of their placement at the end of the pole they become quite important in the speed of the pole moving forward. Softer snow requires larger baskets.

The pole handle should feel comfortable and should have a wider base which holds your hand in the same position — not sliding down the pole as you push off.

The wrist straps often transfer most of the power of your arms to the pole. They should therefore be tight enough to make that transfer. The straps should be leather or nylon. Plastic straps tend to harden in colder temperatures.

A skier of long ago braves bad weather and dangerous terrain with a single pole. The use of poles began about 1500 years ago and solid wood poles came into common use about 100 years ago. Today's poles are much lighter.

The proper length of a pole for classical stride skiing should be to the shoulder. Skating poles will be stiffer and longer (about 15 cm) to allow you to plant the pole behind the push-off ski. Commonly, skating poles reach to about your lower lip. Telemark skiers will use shorter poles, similar to Alpine skiers — with the length of the shaft up to the elbow and the handle coming above the elbow. While standing with your elbow at your side and your lower arm outstretched and parallel to the floor, the proper length pole will just touch the floor when you are holding it in the proper grip.

Adjustable poles are available for those who ski the flats and also descend the steeps.

Clothing

Gaiters are water repellent cloth tubes which fasten under the boots and, depending on their length, reach somewhere between the area above the boot top and just below the knee. They keep snow out of the boot and help to keep the feet warm. They are essential.

Boot covers will keep out water and will keep the feet warm in very cold weather.

All dressed up and no place to go — except the glacier.

Thick wool socks or two pairs of thinner wool socks will keep the feet warm. Norwegians traditionally use long colorful socks that reach above the knee then cover them with knickers which go just below the knee. This older style of dressing is very practical for cross country skiing because long pants are more likely to catch as the legs cross in the stride, and gaiters over long pants become quite bulky while gaiters over long socks are not bulky.

Underclothing should be the type that wicks away the perspiration from the skin. This should never be cotton. Hiking trails are often marked with signs noting that "Cotton kills," because the fabric keeps the moisture close to the body and can cause hypothermia. Several new fabrics wick away the perspiration very well. A wool shirt or sweater will be the next layer. Wool will probably keep you warmest.

Upper body clothing should be in layers. Since skiers generate a great deal of heat, it is easy to perspire. The perspiration then makes them wet, and when resting, the wetness makes them cold. The trick is to take off layers of clothing as the body gets warmer, so that the heat generated by the activity is allowed to escape and the body does not become so hot that you perspire profusely. You will need a wind breaker so that you are not chilled by unexpected winds. Avoid a thick jacket unless you are Telemarking and riding the lifts.

This couple are dressed in the modern type of clothing most skiers wear today. Many Norwegians still dress in the traditional knickers and long socks because they are the most practical of ski clothing.

Mittens or gloves are generally a necessity. Your hands will stay warmer in cross country skiing than in downhill skiing — still, you never want frozen hands. A combination of thin gloves which can be covered by thicker mittens if needed or a good pair of mittens should do.

Head gear is also nearly always required. Whether you wear only ear warmers or a hat, you will need some type of head gear.

Eye protection is always a concern. Both the sun and its reflection off of the snow and the irritant of the wind require good glasses or goggles. Gray or green lenses with ultraviolet ray protection are best for daytime use. Orange or yellow lenses are often better when the sun is setting. These brighter lenses help you to see better when there is no danger of ultraviolet light damage to the eyes.

Sun protection is becoming ever more important as the ozone layer above us breaks up and lets in more harmful ultraviolet cancer-causing rays. Lip and face creams with high sun protective factors, preferably higher than 20, are required. Spring skiing particularly requires attention to the sun because the reflection off the snow can be brutal to your skin.

Care of Equipment

The skis need a flat bottom. If there are cuts and gouges in the base, you will need to use a plastic repair substance such as P-Tex. This is heated, dropped into the depression, then scraped and filed. If the bottom is rough, you can take a metal scraper and run it the length of the ski. The scraper should be periodically sharpened with a file and tested against something which you know is straight — like a T square.

Wax should be removed with an approved wax remover. Klister (a very soft sticky substance that often finds a way to adhere to your clothes, furniture and walls) needs to be scraped off then diluted with cleaning compounds. You will want to do this after every tour, because you don't know what tomorrow's snow conditions may bring. If you had klister on today because it was wet and tomorrow is perfect, you want to be ready to wax and go in the morning.

Always keep a wax coat on your bases. This is particularly important when you put your skis away for the summer. Bases can oxidize and will require much more work the next season to get them back in shape.

Boots need an occasional coating of saddle soap — particularly before being put away for the summer. After every ski tour, it is a good idea to clean off the soles. Dirt and pebbles may be caught in the rough edges of the plastic bottom. If it is plastic you can simply run water over it. The bottom of the boots and the top of the binding foot plate should be sprayed with a Teflon or silicon spray to reduce the ability of snow to cling to it and reduce the efficiency of the meshing of the boot and foot plate.

If You're Going on a Tour

If you are going for a tour, pack your knapsack with some food and drink. You should have some high energy food. In Noway, we use Energel. It is a high energy food made with glucose polymers. These are the fastest absorbed sugars which also aid in water absorption. While you can drink it from the small package, you can also add it to water before you go on your tour. That way you have the best energy source combined with the water necessary to replace the fluids lost in perspiration. (It is not yet available in the U.S.A., so if you want to order a 30 pack case contact Naturkost S. Rui, Box 3036, 1506 Moss, Norway or call 011 47 69 25 87 00 for more information.)

Norwegians like to make a day of skiing, so they always bring a lunch — and drinks. Warm drinks are especially delicious during a long day of skiing. You should also bring a lightweight foam cushion. Sunscreen is a necessity as are lip sun blocks. Of course you will want to bring your scraper (to remove unwanted ice or wax), some waxes and a cork to rub the wax in. Make sure that your backpack is large enough to carry all you need and still have room to store the clothes you shed as you warm up.

10

Waxing and Base Preparation for Nordic Skiing

It seems that for many skiers half of the challenge is in determining the correct wax, then waxing the skis effectively. The better wax companies spend a great deal of time and money developing and testing waxes. This has allowed them to continually improve the durability of the wax, increase the temperature range for which the wax is appropriate, and to make waxes last longer. Swix, now in its 50th year, is the leader in this field. We appreciate the assistance given in the preparation of this chapter by Harald Bjerke of Swix in Lillehammer and by his research staff.

The major obstacle for a skier to overcome is the friction of the snow — the adhesion of the snow to the base of the ski and the unevenness of the snow surface which requires that the ski "plows through" the snow. The "structure" cut into the ski base and the wax chosen increases the ability to push off with the power leg. At the same time the wax chosen for the gliding phase should reduce the friction or suction between the ski and the water under the ski. The pressure of the ski on the snow creates friction which heats and melts the snow so the skier is usually skiing on a thin coat of water. This is more prevalent during warm weather since there is more water between the particles of snow.

If you want to rank the importance of each element in terms of glide and friction, we evaluate them this way: The skis (flex, base, stiffness, etc.) are most important in terms of speed. For classical skiers the next most important factor is the kick wax. Then there is a great drop in importance to the third factor, the "structure" (which will be discussed later in this chapter), then last, the glide wax. If you are a skater, there is no kick wax so the ski is far and away the most important, followed by the structure, then the glide wax. Of course, for world class racers each is very important.

You might be interested to know that when we go to a World Cup event each skier will bring 10 to 12 pairs of skis for the different conditions which might be encountered. Vladimir Shmirnov, the great Russian skier, currently the second best in the world, may bring 30 pairs of skis to an event. But he has two men to handle his equipment. We would bring that many if we could, but the transportation costs are too great.

Waxes are generally made from hydrocarbon waxes, such as paraffin, mixed with other waxes. Graphite and fluorocarbons are also used in many of the newer waxes. Harder waxes are made from a mixture of the hydrocarbon waxes with other waxes of varying density. Waxes composed of larger molecules are harder than those with smaller molecules. The harder waxes will feel dry when applied. The softer waxes will feel tacky.

The harder waxes are for colder weather. The softer the wax, the more it is used for higher temperatures. Which to use? First check the outside temperature. This will give you an idea. If the temperature is over 34 degrees (1 degree Celsius), the snow will probably be wet. If it is less than 25 degrees (4 degrees Celsius), it should be dry so a harder wax will work. If it is between these two temperatures, try the hand test. Take a handful of snow and squeeze it. If it clumps together in a ball it is wet, it if does not compact and stays loose it is dry. The wet snow is warmer, the dry snow is colder.

Since the water content of snow varies with altitude and geographical area, the temperature range shown on the wax may not be exact for the snow on which you are skiing. The same temperature in Oslo, Mammoth, Portland or St. Paul may require slightly different waxes to give you maximum skiing performance. You may have to experiment a bit and move up or down one or two colors to get the perfect wax for your tour.

Generally it is best to wax for the coldest snow you expect. The soft wax, used for the warmer snow, will often ice up and stop sliding. So if you have used too soft a wax you may have to stop in midtrail, clean the skis and rewax.

You should do your waxing indoors where the ski and wax are warmer and more workable. The skis must be clean and dry for best results. It is also best to clean your skis indoors. It is preferable to clean the skis after each day's skiing. Do this by taking your plastic scraper and peeling off the excess wax. Then use a ski cleaner to finish the job. Always do a good job of cleaning before you put the skis away for the summer. If you are feeling lazy, you can leave on wax for a day or two but take off the klister!

Choosing the Right Wax

All the beginner needs to know is the outside air temperature, then select a wax which is appropriate for that temperature. If you are skiing the classical diagonal stride technique, you will select a kick wax and a glide wax. If you are skating, you will select only a glide wax. As you become more advanced, other factors may also be taken into consideration. In this chapter, we will discuss waxing for beginners as well as for advanced skiers and racers. So read on if you want to know more of the technical details. Or, just check the boxes at the end of the chapter for the step-by-step instructions for whatever you want to do.

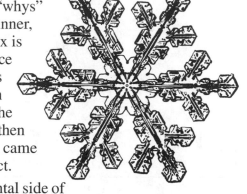

As you become more interested in top performance, you will want to know more of the "whys" and "hows" of waxing. But even as a beginner, you will want to understand why your wax is dragging or is too slippery. Was it your choice of wax or was it your technique? Waxing is both an art and a science. And luck often plays a part, too. You may have chosen the perfect wax for the beginning of your tour, then it snowed, or the wind came up, or the sun came out — and your wax was no longer perfect.

You might say that waxing is the mental side of your skiing. It is like chess. You are playing against Mother Nature — and you won't always win. That's why skiers discuss waxing far more often than technique.

Humidity is important, but only in a general sense. If a climate is particularly dry, below 50 percent humidity, you will use one wax. If the humidity is higher than 50 percent, you can assume that the air temperature is 1 to 4 degrees higher on the Fahrenheit scale (½ to 2 degrees Celsius), so you will use a softer wax. If the humidity is 100 percent it is snowing!

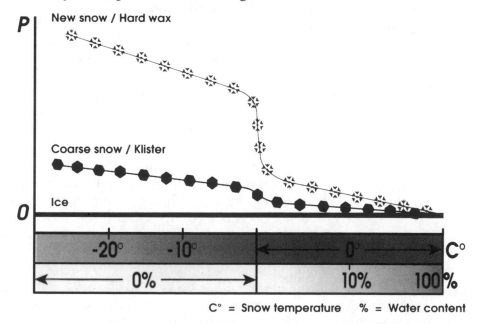

Penetration levels of ice and snow as a function of snow temperature and water content (shown on a logarithmic scale). The greater penetration (P) requires a harder wax while no penetration (O) requires soft wax or klister.

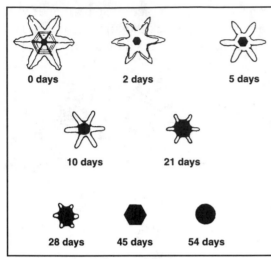

0 days   **2 days**   **5 days**

10 days   **21 days**

28 days   **45 days**   **54 days**

Types of Snow

Snow granulation varies from the large six-pointed or six-sided crystals of newly fallen snow to nearly round crystals of month-old snow. According to Kenneth Aasheim, perhaps the world's most sought after ski technician, there are over 30 different kinds of snow crystals.

For the sharp crystals of new snow, you will want a hard wax which will resist the penetration of the snow into the base. When the snow is warmer and wetter, the wax chosen must have good water repelling properties. It will be a softer wax.

It is much easier to wax for old snow than for new snow. Old snow will have similar characteristics no matter where you are. But new snow varies in terms of dryness, size of flakes and other characteristics each of which takes a different wax or technique in order to deal with the friction variations. The quality of snow also varies from area to area. So for maximum waxing effectiveness, you may have to experiment to find the very best approach to the snow you are skiing.

Heat transfer from the snow relates to both the temperature and the humidity. These factors are, of course, continually changing. If the humidity is high, there is more condensation of water on to the snow. A softer wax is therefore required. But if the air is dry, the molecules go from a solid state to gas without first becoming water, so a harder wax than the temperature would indicate should be used.

Wind is another variable in proper wax selection. The wind tends to tighten the smaller snow particles which makes more of the snow come in contact with the ski base. This increases friction. A harder (colder temperature) wax is called for.

Reflection (albedo) is an often overlooked condition. The snow can absorb energy from the sun, or on cloudy days, the heat from the earth can be reflected back by the clouds and absorbed by the snow. In either case, there can be a warming. A low angle of the sun or a cover of dry clean snow may result in almost no energy being absorbed by the snow. But a high sun or dirty or wet snow can absorb as much as 65 percent of the sun's rays.

The resultant snow friction is a combination of the above factors, plus the amount of heat generated by the friction of the ski as it passes over the snow and the unevenness of the snow (you know, when you have to plow through the trail). Temperature, of course, is a primary ingredient.

■ Wet snow friction occurs when the temperature is above freezing, and it is aided by higher humidity or more sun absorption.

94

- Intermediate snow friction is when temperatures are 32 to 10 degrees (0 to -12 C).

- Dry snow friction occurs at the colder temperatures (below 10 degrees F or -12 degrees C). It is aided by less humidity, less heat absorption and more wind.

Base Preparation

Normal preparation is performed at the factory. This preparation can include either sanding or stone grinding (the preferable method). Sanding tends to rip up small strips of the base. These have to be removed at some point in order for the ski to get maximum glide. Stone grinding cuts the base and doesn't leave these fibers or "hairs."

For advanced skiers and racers, additional base preparation may be desired. You may want to do it or have a technician handle the job. In the whole world, there are only three or four top technicians with the proper equipment to do the job right. But most technicians can outperform the amateur doing the job at home. After the base preparation or "structure" is complete, you will certainly want to wax your own skis.

Tools and Accessories for Base Preparation and Waxing

Tomm Murstad's shop in Holmenkollen is generally considered the best in the world. People the world over send their skis to him for the finest work. He is used by both Alpine and Nordic teams from as far away as Australia and Japan, nearly all of the European national teams, and of course, the United States downhill and cross country teams. (For you serious skiers interested in having him handle your skis, he can be reached at Tryvannsveien 2, Oslo 0394, Norway. Phone from the USA, 011-47-22-14-41-24.) The cost for a new base structure is $40 to $50, plus the shipping charges for the skis.

If you want to do it yourself and have a well-equipped tool shop, you may have most of what you need. If not, here are some of the tools which you may find helpful. We have used the Swix code numbers so that you have an idea of what to order. Many of these tools are also available from other sources.

Waxing Table

A waxing table is necessary so that you can work with your skis comfortably. Your own workbench, a high, stable table, a Black and Decker bench, or the Swix T 76 all work well.

Waxing Table

Detailed enlargement (x500) of untreated racing base.

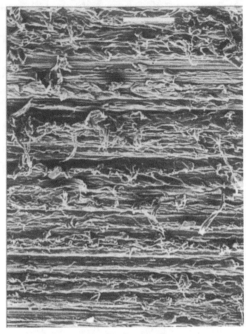

The same untreated base (x100).

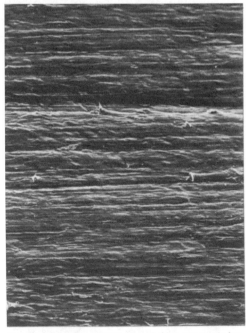

Stone-grinded ski base (x100). Remarkable improvement but still some micro-burrs left.

Final result after stone-grinding, treatment by T180 riller-bar, and Fibertex (x100).

Enlarged pictures of bases

Vises

Vises are required to hold the skis. The Swix (T146X) is built especially for skis and has a lip which holds the ski solidly; you should have two such vises. A support vise is also desirable to hold up the middle of the ski and reduce the bend. (Swix T 78)

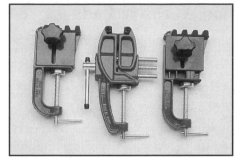

Vises

An Iron

There are special irons made particularly for skis, but any old iron will do. An electric iron is highly desirable. The Swix T 7311 or T 7322 make it easier to select the proper temperatures for efficient waxing. If you are using an old clothes iron, be certain that it is not too hot. If the wax smokes, the iron is too hot. Turn the gauge down until there is no smoking.

Ski Iron

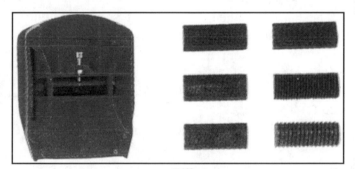

Rillers

Riller

A riller is necessary to prepare ski bases for waxing. A rill is a long valley. The riller makes long grooves in your ski bases. You can use the edge of a file to rill your bases, but you will get much better results with a professional tool. These tools generally come in several gauges, from the very fine 0.33 mm to the very course 3 mm blades (T401, T401XF, T401F, T401M, T401G, T401-2 and T401-3). The gauge of the rill tells how far apart the rills will be. Deeper rills for wetter snow will be developed with more pressure on the tool.

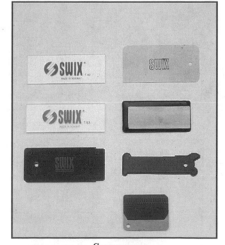

Scrapers

Scrapers

Scrapers are made of plastic or metal and are used to smooth the base or clean the grooves.

Nylon Abrasive Pads

These pads, such as Swix Fibertex or Scotch-Brite, are used to remove burrs created by rilling.

Sandpaper

You need several grades of sandpaper: from 320 (very fine) through 100 (most commonly used); and 60 (coarse) for wet snow.

Base Cleaner

The base cleaner can be any of the traditional solvents and wax removers which are usually made from petroleum products. Swix has a citrus-based cleaner which is more environmentally sound (Swix I72, I74, I77). But since some people are allergic to citrus products, rubber or plastic gloves should be used.

Solvent Impregnated Towels

These towels, like those made of Swix Fiberlene™, are very handy for assisting in cleaning the ski bases.

Wax Brushes

- Stiff horsehair brushes (T157) are used by racers. This type spreads the wax and removes the excess.
- Use hard bristle nylon brushes (such as Swix T161) for the initial brushing of waxes.
- Soft bristle nylon brushes (T160) are used for the final brushing of wax.
- Mixed fiber brushes (T155) remove all waxes and are especially good for harder waxes.
- Rotary brushes are used with electric drills.

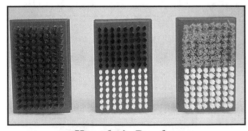
Horsehair Brushes

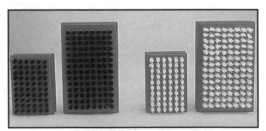
Hard Bristle Nylon Brushes

Soft Bristle Nylon Brushes

Rotary Brushes are used with Electric Drills

Cork

A flat cork hand piece, such as the T20, is needed for rubbing in the wax.

Corks

Safety Precautions

Most waxes, such as Swix, are quite safe to work with as long as they are not exposed to an open flame or you are not using power tools which will create a dust which can be inhaled. Smaller wax companies may not have the testing potentials of the larger companies and may use a lower grade of fluorocarbon wax, which may increase the hazards. Check the package to make certain that you have read the required precautionary warnings and the guidelines for application.

When environmentally conscious skiers see the word fluorocarbon, they generally think of the chlorofluorocarbon (CFC) gases which pollute the atmosphere. However, tests show that the fluorocarbons in the waxes are quite inert and pose no threat to the environment.

For your safety, consider these precautions when waxing:

1) Work in a well ventilated area. You must have a fresh air supply, and there should be exhaust fans to evacuate the gases from the waxes.

2) Keep waxes away from open flames, such as waxing torches, space heaters and heat guns. Also, don't smoke while waxing skis. While all waxes can pose a danger, fluorocarbon waxes are potentially the most dangerous. At temperatures over 570 degrees Fahrenheit, or 300 Celsius, fluorocarbons disintegrate and become highly poisonous gases. Normal ironing of the waxes does not create this much heat.

3) Using power brushes to brush on your wax increases the occurrence of small wax particles (wax dust). To reduce this danger, use a paper mask such as is used when working with wood.

4) Use safety glasses when power brushing.

5) Be aware of the flammable character of the solvents you use to clean. Dispose of the rags or Fiberlene (solvent treated paper-like toweling) promptly.

6) Because of the flammability of the fluorocarbons added to hard waxes and klisters, they must not be exposed to open flames. Waxing torches should not be used for applying or removing fluorinated kick waxes. Irons are fine for applying such waxes, but solvents must be used when removing them.

Preparing the Base Structure of Your Skis

Serious skiers will usually rill their bases. Rilling sets grooves into the bottom of the base, which helps to reduce the suction of the water formed under the ski when the pressure of the ski melts the snow under it. You can also rill your wax after you have waxed the ski. Skaters and those skiing on wet snow are most likely to profit by rilling in order to get the maximum glide.

To improve glide you will want texture "structures" on the base of your skis. This will allow less of the base of the ski to come in contact with the snow, and it will reduce the surface tension of the water under the ski. Skis come from the factory with a structure. This may be good enough for you, or you may want to change the structure because of the snow conditions. A good ski technician is the person to turn to in this case. However, some people prefer to do their own structures — it's cheaper and more personal. You can attain a certain intimacy with your skis. Some skiers therefore do not want to let another touch their skis.

The structure from the factory won't last forever. As your bases age and as snow conditions change, a new structure may be in order. Top racers will have their skis restructured two or more times per year. Bases in need of a new or an improved structure include those which are:

- very shiny.

- have a sealed surface from high heat or high pressure base finish from the factory.

- have oxidized or dry bases caused by excessive exposure to the elements without being protected by wax.

The type of "structure" desired varies with the amount of friction which the snow will produce. This depends on the amount of water under the ski as the ski passes over it. Dry snow will have only the water that is caused by the pressure of the ski. Wet snow will already have a good deal of water that is increased as the pressure of the ski compresses it. The wet snow creates more suction and increases the drag of the snow.

- For dry snow (5 degrees F, -15 C or colder), you will want a fine structure — very small grooves.

- For intermediate snow friction (5 to 32 degrees F, 0 to -15 C), you will want a medium structure.

- For wet snow (32 degrees F or 0 degrees C or warmer), you will want a course structure (deeper grooves to allow the water to flow more easily).

Professional preparation is usually your best bet. Let a ski technician structure your skis at the beginning of the season and during the season as the snow conditions change. The technician will generally use machines such as belt sanders or grinders. Stone grinders are far better.

While a straight series of rills from tip to toe is quite common, Kenneth Aashein of Tomm Murstad's Skiservice, perhaps the world's foremost technician, tells us that of the eight base structures which they use, the diagonal rills or the crossing diagonal rills are most effective. The latter structure, which forms thousands of diamond patterns on the ski base, is most often used by both Nordic and Alpine skiers. The double diagonal pattern has the rills going in one direction slightly deeper than those going the other direction. Thousands of tests indicate that this is the best known pattern today — but the research continues. Eventually scientists and technicians may discover the "best" type of structure for each of the more than 30 types of snow crystals, but for now we are looking for just a few all-purpose structures.

The machines which make the modern structure patterns with special stone grinding patterns cost about $160,000. So it is not likely that you will have one lying around the garage. At Tomm Murstad's, the workroom which is used only for preparing ski bases and applying structures is about 25 by 90 feet and contains 10 machines that handle different parts of the process for repairing or finishing skis. Of course, this is the world's largest ski service shop with 6 to 10 technicians working full time.

If you do your own skis, it is most likely that you will use hand tools. Your rills will run only from tip to toe. Choose the proper depth of the rills (grooves) you want on your skis — from 0.25 mm for very hard snow to 3 mm for very wet snow. Support the entire length of the ski with a profile type vise (such as the Swix T79).

With a constant pressure, rill the ski from tip to tail. You can use a single structure (depth of grooves), or you can use a combination of structures, both deep and shallow. After rilling the base, use a scraper to remove the parts (the fibers or hairs) of the base which have been lifted by the rilling. After scraping, use Fibertex (Swix T265) or a similar substance to smooth the surface even more so that only the base and the rills remain — no extra scrapings or dust. Any

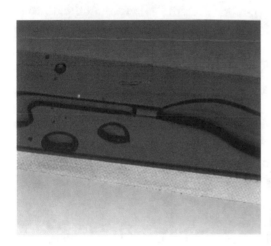

Left: High Water Repellancy

Right: Low Water Repellancy

microfibers or hairs left on the base will limit its gliding potential. You can then finish with a softer abrasive, such as Swix T266, moving only in the tip to tail direction. (Box A)

Box A

Structuring the Ski Base:

1) Support the entire length of the ski with a profile type vise (such as the Swix T79).

2) Choose the proper depth of the rills (grooves) you want on your skis — from 0.25 mm for very hard snow to 3.0 mm for very wet snow.

3) Rill the ski from tip to tail using a firm and constant pressure. You can use a single structure (depth of grooves), or you can use a combination of structures, both deep and shallow.

4) Use a scraper to remove the parts of the base which have been lifted by the rilling.

5) Smooth the surface even more using Fibertex (Swix T265) or a similar substance so that only the base and the rills remain — no extra scrapings or dust. Work the Fibertex both up and down the ski so that no fibers remain.

6) Finish with a softer abrasive, such as Swix T266, moving only in the tip to tail direction.

Wax Hardness and Color Coding

The waxes vary from the very soft klisters, which contain little or no actual wax, to the hard waxes. Each wax or klister is recommended for certain temperature ranges and snow conditions. The warmer colors (yellow and red) are for warmer temperatures. Purple, the combination of red and blue, is next. The blues are for the cold, the greens for still colder temperatures. The following list includes color waxes from several manufacturers, but will give you an idea of what is available.

Green

Green is the hardest wax (20 to 3 degrees F, -7 to -15 C). It is for very cold conditions, as well as new or fine grained snow. This wax is to be used in the warmer range of the recommended temperatures (near 20 degrees F or -7 C); the humidity should be low.

Blue

Blue is a slightly softer wax. The recommended temperatures are 21 to 30 degrees F (-1 to -6 C). If the humidity is higher than 80 percent, it is snowing, or the snow is older, it can be used at temperatures several degrees lower than those recommended.

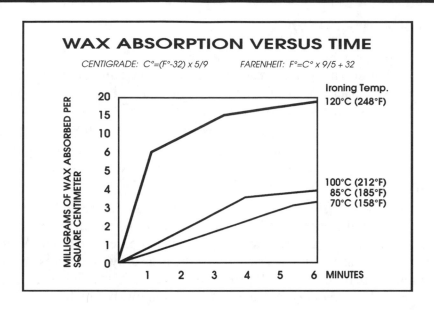

WAX ABSORPTION VERSUS TIME

CENTIGRADE: C°=(F°-32) x 5/9   *FARENHEIT: F°=C° x 9/5 + 32*

MILLIGRAMS OF WAX ABSORBED PER SQUARE CENTIMETER

Ironing Temp.
120°C (248°F)

100°C (212°F)
85°C (185°F)
70°C (158°F)

MINUTES

Violet

Violet is softer still and is recommended for 30 to 32 degrees F (0 to -1 C). It can be used down to 25 degrees F (-4 C) if the humidity is high or snow is falling.

Pink

Pink is often used as a base coat. As a final wax it is best in the 34 to 21 degree F range (+1 to -6 C).

Red

Red is just a bit softer than the violet. Its recommended temperature range is 32 to 34 degrees F (0 to +1 C). While its primary function is to be effective just above freezing, it will work well a few degrees lower without icing up.

Silver

Silver is for moist, new snow and falling snow, from 32 to 36 degrees F (0 to +2 C). It can be layered with other waxes to reduce icing.

Yellow

Yellow (Klisterwax) is for 34 to 41 degrees F (+2 to +5 C). This very tacky klister gets a grip on wet or "glazed" snow. Actually, the composition of the snow is more important than the temperature. Wet snow which has been skied and has developed a shiny mirror-like glaze is the condition for which klister is used most often. Swix yellow fluorocarbon waxes generally have temperature ranges from 32 to 50 degrees F (0 to +10 C).

White

White is the softest wax. It is often made of a silicon formula. The temperature range is 36 to 59 degrees F (+2 to +15 C).

The above list is not all encompassing. For example, Swix makes four graphite waxes for use in low humidity situations. The color codes for the graphite waxes do not match the above temperatures for the same colors.

Waxing Your Skis

To prepare a new ski, melt in a sealer wax, such as a Swix orange, then polish or cork it in. This will increase the life of the base and give a better surface for other waxes to adhere to. If the base is a bit rough, as is sometimes true for polyethylene bases, a paraffin coat can seal it effectively. (Box B)

Often after you have used a ski on hard snow, you will have damaged the base. This is called "base burn." While it looks smooth, it actually is quite rough — microscopically speaking. Base burned skis and oxidized bases require this same type of preparation before waxing.

For maximum efficiency, the ski bottoms should be treated especially for the use for which they are intended — ice, warm snow, etc. In 1993 the Norwegian wax coach had 70 different ways to prepare ski base structures. We may all be getting too technical at every level! Now he uses only three: crossing, diagonal or diamond patterns. One is for wet snow, over 1 degree Celsius; one type is for snow exactly at freezing; and another for dry snow, below freezing.

Preparing Older Skis

To prepare an older ski for waxing, first scrape off old wax with a base scraper and with a groove scraper. Next brush with a hard brush, then a softer brush — brush from tip to tail. Repair any damaged spots by using a polyethylene stick (such as Swix Polystick T170). From the burning stick, drop as much hot polyethylene as needed into the damaged area. After allowing it to cool, scrape off the excess with a steel scraper or a file, then sand with No. 220 sandpaper.

Box B

Preparing a new ski or an older oxidized base which has been restructured:

1) Melt in a sealer wax, such as a Swix orange and polish or cork it in. This will increase the life of the base and give a better surface for other waxes to adhere to.

2) If the base is a bit rough, as is sometimes true for polyethylene bases, a paraffin coat can seal it effectively.

3) Scrape off old wax with a base scraper and with a groove scraper.

4) Brush with a hard brush, then a softer brush — brush from tip to tail.

5) Repair any damaged spots by using a polyethylene stick (such as Swix Polystick T170). From the burning stick drop as much hot polyethylene as needed into the damaged area. After allowing it to cool, scrape off the excess with a steel scraper or a file. Sand with No. 220 sandpaper.

6) Smooth the side edges with a steel scraper.

Box C

Preparing older skis:

1) Scrape off old wax with a base scraper and with a groove scraper.

2) Brush with a hard brush, then a softer brush — brushing from tip to tail.

3) Repair any damaged spots by using a polyethylene stick (such as Swix Polystick T170). From the burning stick, drop as much hot polyethylene as needed into the damaged area. After allowing it to cool, scrape off the excess with a steel scraper or a file. Sand with No. 220 sandpaper.

4) Smooth the side edges with a steel scraper.

5) If new structuring is required, rerill the ski base. (See Box A)

6) Scrape the ski base with a razor blade scraper to remove any excess left from the rilling.

7) Fibertex the ski base to remove excess fibers, dust and oxidation.

Now smooth the side edges with a steel scraper. (Box C)

If the base needs a new structure, rerill the ski base. Remove the burrs and microfibers from the ski base with a razor blade scraper. Fibertex the ski base to remove excess fibers, dust and oxidation. (See Box A.)

For Recreational Touring

If you are waxing for a recreational tour, clean the base with a solvent or solvent impregnated towels. Choose the proper wax or waxes (Boxes E-1, skating; or E-2, classical). Classic skiers may use only a kick wax, or they may use a glide wax on the front and back of the bases. Skaters will use a glide wax the whole length of the ski. (See Box B.)

Classic, diagonal stride skiers have different needs than do skaters. Each will use different waxes and different waxing techniques. Let's start with the classical skiers.

The "Wax Pocket" or "Kick Zone"

This is the area which will have your kick or grip wax. It is the area which will be in contact with the snow when you have most of your weight on one ski.

First you must find your "kick zone." This is the area under your boot which will come in contact with the snow when you push off. The kick zone for dry snow will normally be about 16 to 20 inches (40 to 50 cm). The front end of the zone will begin 8 to 12 inches (20 to 30 cm) in front of the toe piece of the binding. If you are using klister for wet snow, the zone will be shortened to reduce the chance of it dragging during the glide. It will be about 14 to 18 inches long (35 to 45 cm) and will begin about 8 inches (20 cm) front of the binding. In either case the zone will not extend as far back as the end of the binding but will end 2 to 4 inches (5 to 10 cm) in front of the heel of the binding — about even with the heel of your boot. Sometimes the two skis have slightly different pocket areas. To find the wax pocket you can do the paper test again. (It is described in Chapter 9 on equipment.) Or you can put the ski bases together, then pull the arched middle sections of the skis together with one hand. When the air gap between them is about 20 inches (50 cm) long, mark the two ends of the air gap, and you will have your wax pocket. If the snow is particularly icy and you want more control and less speed, you may wax more than the wax pocket — perhaps waxing the whole ski bottom.

The above tests give you a pretty good idea of where the normal kick zone is. However, for you, the exact kick zone may be slightly different. The exact length of the kick zone is determined by several factors such as: the flex of the ski, the weight of the skier, the skier's technique and the condition of the snow. To determine the maximum kick zone for yourself, wax an area from the back of the binding forward about 30 inches (75 cm). Ski for a while. You should have a good grip, but your glide will probably be less than desirable. Then take a scraper and shave back about an inch. Ski again. Repeat the "ski-then-shave" pattern until you have reached a point where you have both good grip and good glide. Mark the wax zone on the side of your ski.

Remember that the shorter the kicking zone, the better the glide. If you are very strong, with a strong kick and/or a strong poling action, or if you have an exceptionally good technique, you may be able to use a shorter kick zone. But for beginners and children, it is best to use a long kick zone.

Prewax the Kick Zone

First, you will prewax the kick zone (base waxing) so that it will better handle the kick waxes which you will later apply. If you are working on classical skis, define the kick zone. Sand that area up and down the ski with No. 100 sandpaper. Coat the kick zone with a soft penetrating wax, such as Swix CH10, then iron it in. The ironing opens the pores of the base of the ski and allows a greater penetration of the wax. It will therefore last longer.

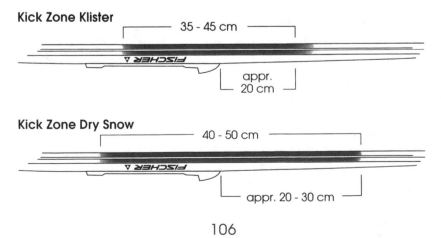

Kick Zone Klister

35 - 45 cm

FISCHER

appr. 20 cm

Kick Zone Dry Snow

40 - 50 cm

FISCHER

appr. 20 - 30 cm

> ## Box D
>
> ### Base Waxing to protect the base and make other waxes last longer:
>
> 1) Sand the kick zone, lengthwise, with No. 100 sandpaper.
> 2) Remove any fibers with Fibertex or a Plexi Scraper.
> 3) Iron in a thin layer of wax. Let it cool.
> 4) Apply 2 or 3 additional thin layers, and cork each one smooth. (Never wax the kick zone with gliding wax.)
> 5) Brush with a sufficiently stiff brush to clear the rills.

Using a scraper, scrape the wax while the wax is still hot. Reapply the same wax and allow it to cool. Scrape it again. Repeat this process at least three times. Brush off the wax with a hard brush, such as the hard nylon Swix T161. Brush from front to rear. Use a softer brush, such as the mixed fiber T155. The brushing reduces the amount of wax in the rills so that the structure will be effective. If you filled the rills with wax, you would get no effect from the structure which was applied. Then use Fibertex and a sharp razor blade type scraper (T89) to cut remaining microfibers. (See Box D.)

Kick Waxes

There is both an art and a science to waxing. In fact, waxing your skis may be the biggest challenge of the day. Now that you have the kick zone ready for the "wax of the day," you must accurately answer several questions in order to choose the best wax. There are a number of factors which must be taken into account.

Waxing for Grip

This technique is performed by all classical skiers. First find the wax pocket then select the proper wax. The proper wax depends on two variables — the temperature and the condition of the snow — whether it is new or old, wet or dry, loose or packed. Kick waxes come in two general categories. The older type is made from hydrocarbons and other petroleum derivatives. The newer type is made from fluorocarbon lubricants that increase gliding capabilities, reduce icing and better resist pollutants which may be in the snow.

New snow is made from the six-sided crystals or the familiar six-pointed crystal which you see on so many Christmas cards. Since it is "sharp" it will tend to grip the ski base, so a hard wax which will prevent this penetration will be best. After the snow has melted, it becomes more like a little ball. It therefore has reduced gripping power, because it is part snow and part water. So you will need a soft wax to grip the snow. If you use a wax that is too soft for the snow, it will pick up the snow and the ski will stick. You will then have to scrape the snow off the bottom of the ski and perhaps even rewax the ski with a harder wax.

Box E-1

Glide Wax Chart for Racers and Advanced Skiers

A more concrete example of the number of Swix waxes available to you is shown in the following chart. There are four levels of categories for its waxes. The color codes are the same for categories 2, 3 and 4, but the uses vary depending on the conditions.

Category 1

FC are pure wax powders. These are the closest waxes to being a universal "one-wax-fits-all" wax.

- Cera FC200 is a high level racing wax for temperatures from +15 to -4 degrees Celsius (25 to 60 degrees Fahrenheit).
- Cera FC 100 is for colder conditions 0 to -15 C (32 to 5 degrees F).

Category 2

HF (high fluorocarbon) waxes for fast acceleration, wide temperature range; used for high humidity or wet conditions. Generally used with a Category 1 (Cera F) wax as an overlayer.

HF 4 Blue

- -10 to -30 degrees C (-25 to 14 F).
- High humidity, over 80 percent with very cold temperature.
- No need to use an overlayer.

HF 6 Violet

- -4 to -10 C (+14 to +25 F).
- Abrasive manmade snow.
- Use FC 100 as an overlayer.

HF 8 Pink

- -6 to +1 C (+21 to +34 F) — use as an iron base coat
- Use overlayer of FC 100 or 200 (depending on the temperature)

HF 10 Yellow

- 0 to +10 C (+32 to +50 F)
- For very wet conditions (falling wet snow, rain, wet surface snow)
- Use with FC 200 as an overlayer

Category 3

LF (low fluorocarbon); used in low humidity, dry conditions.

LF 4 Blue

- -10 to -32 C (-25 to +14 F)
- Use with very cold temperatures and/or harsh man made snow.
- No need for an overlayer unless humidity is higher or the temperature range is at the high end, then use an overlayer of FC 100.

LF 6 Violet

- -10 to -4 C (+14 to +25 F)
- Can be used alone or as a base coat for other waxes

LF 8 Pink

- -6 to +1 C (+21 to +34 F)
- For racing use a Category 1 FC wax (depending on the temperature) as an overlayer

LF 10 Yellow

- 0 to +10 C (32 to 50 F)
- Because snow may be dirty, an overlayer of FC 200 is recommended
- Can be used as a base protecting wax when storing or traveling to avoid oxidation

Category 4

Hydrocarbon waxes with no fluorocarbon additives. These are more economical and more often used by recreational skiers.

CH 4 Ice Blue

- -32 to -10 C (-25 to 14 F)
- This is the hardest wax of all.
- Can be mixed with other waxes to increase durability on ice.

CH 6 Violet

- -10 to -4 C (+14 to +25 F)
- Particularly good for summer skiing on glaciers

CH 8 Pink

- -6 to +1 C (21 to 34 F)
- Good base preparation wax and travel wax to protect bases

CH 10 Yellow

- 0 to +10 C (32 to 50 F)
- Use FC 200 as an overlayer
- Good base preparation and travel wax

CH 11 Silicone White

- +2 to +15 C (36 to 59 F)
- Softest of all of the waxes
- Particularly suited for the wetter conditions of coastal mountains where the snow is often wet.

Graphite Waxes

Graphite waxes are a combination of graphite with a high fluorocarbon (HF) or a low fluorocarbon (LF) wax. These waxes are often ideal in low humidity situations (less than 50 percent). They help to reduce the penetration of the sharp snow crystals into the base or the wax.

HFG 8 (High fluorocarbon graphite) Black

- -6 to +1 C (21 to 34 F)
- Used with "dry glaze" conditions — low humidity, high sun radiation (new snow and warmer temperatures, such as may occur at higher elevations later in the year).
- Generally mixed with nongraphite wax.

LFG 4 (Low fluorocarbon graphite) Blue

- -32 to -10 C (-25 to +14 F) — very cold, low humidity wax
- Often used as a base wax for other waxes
- Seldom use an overcoat of Category 1 wax

LFG 6 Violet

- -10 to -4 C (14 to 25 F)
- Low humidity counterpart for HF 6 or LF 6
- Good base layer for another race wax
- Often used without an overcoat of Category 1 wax

LFG 8 Pink
- -6 to +1 C (21 to 34 F)
- Low humidity counterpart to HF 8 and LF 8
- Usually used with other waxes
- Use Category 1 wax as an overcoat

The temperature has similar effects. Very cold weather will keep the snow in its crystalline form — sharp. Warmer temperatures will melt the snow easily with the friction of the ski. So warmer temperatures will require a softer wax or a very soft sticky "klister." High humidity such as fog will also make the snow wetter. Conversely, wind will often dry the snow possibly requiring a harder wax than the temperature indicates.

You have already put on one coat of base wax, such as VF Orange. Now select the kick wax you want. (If you are using klister, don't use a base coat of wax.) The Swix Cera Classic line of waxes should serve you well. Refer to Box E-2 for the appropriate temperature ranges.

Box E-2

Kick Waxes

There are three categories of kick waxes: the traditional hydrocarbon waxes used commonly by recreational skiers and the high and low percent fluorocarbon mixes used primarily for racing. The kick waxes are more difficult to judge correctly, because they have small temperature ranges, much smaller than the gliding waxes. This is particularly true when the temperature is around zero.

XF (High fluorocarbon waxes)
XF 20 Green
- -18 to -5 C (3 to 23 F)
- Hardest of the kick waxes
- For use with fine grained snow or new snow
- If this wax is used in the warmer temperature range, the humidity should be low.

XF 30 Blue
- -6 to -1 C (+21 to 32 F)
- This covers most normal snow conditions
- If the humidity is higher than 80 percent or the snow is older, it can be used at several degrees lower than the recommended temperature.

XF 40 Violet
- -1 to 0 C (30 to 32 F)
- In high humidity or falling snow, the XF 30 (above) may be slippery so this wax will be more effective.

XF 50 Red
- 0 to +1 C (32 to 34 F)
- Can be used with slightly colder snow without icing.

XF 60 Silver
- 0 to +2 C (32 to 36 F)
- For moist new snow and falling snow
- Resists icing so can be applied over other waxes in a thin coat to reduce icing problems.

XF 70 Yellow
- +2 to +5 C (34 to 41 F)
- This is a tacky almost klister-type wax.
- Used for warmer temperatures and a more granular snow.
- If there is a "glazed" condition, fresh wet snow which is becoming shiny or mirror-like when skied, this is the wax. The conditions outside of the tracks may be quite different, so look at the tracks.

Cera Classic VF Line (Variable to low percentage fluorocarbons)
VF 20 Green/blue
- -7 C (19 F)
- For new snow with low humidity

VF 30 Blue
- -1 to -8 C (18 to 30 F)
- A flexible wax which covers many snow conditions

VF 40 Blue/violet
- 0 to -1 C (30 to 32 F)
- To be used if VF 30 is slippery
- Can be used at lower temperatures if air is moist, such as with snowfall or fog

VF 50 Violet/red
- 0 to +2 C (32 to 36 F)
- For moist snow, new or falling snow

VF 60 Red/silver
- +1 to +5 C (34 to 41 F)
- A versatile wax for new wet snow
- Can be used for very wet snow in the sun to colder fine grained snow in the shadows.

VF 80 Orange
- -15 to 0 C (5 to 32 F)
- An outstanding base wax
- Particularly useful when the snow is abrasive
- To use as a base, apply to the kick zone, cork it smooth, iron it in, cork again.

Klisters

Used for a better grip on wet or course grain (melted and refrozen) hard snow

KF 2
- -5 to +5 C (23 to 50 F)
- A universal klister

KF 3 Red special
- 0 to +3 C (32 to 38 F)
- Use for good snow that is somewhat wet and course grained, which is not fully saturated with water.

KF 4 Red
- +2 C (37 F)
- For old wet snow

KF 5 Silver
- 0 C (32 F)
- Less tacky because of metal particles in the klister
- Often blended with other klisters

If you are waxing for the kick zone, first sand the base wax with No. 100 sandpaper to improve the bond between it and the kick wax. Apply the appropriate kick wax (See Box E-2.) by rubbing it on to the kick zone. Cork or iron it in. Ironing is better. Then apply two or three additional layers, and cork each into the ironed wax. Three or four thin layers are better than one thick layer, which is difficult to cork smooth. Leaving the wax rough does not improve the grip, but will reduce the glide. If you need a better grip, use a softer wax.

For cold weather or new snow, choose the wax which you think will do the job. (You should have several waxes available — preferably from the same manufacturer.) If you are not sure of which wax to use, go with the harder wax first. Wax at room temperature where the wax will work into the skis more effectively. The colder the snow, the thinner the wax coat should be. For harder snows and colder temperatures rub on the wax as if you were coloring the base with a crayon. Work to make the wax penetrate into the ski base by heat (ironing) or by pressure (corking it in). The longer the race, the more individual layers of wax you will need. (See Box F for simple recreational tour waxing; Box G for more complicated race waxing; Box H for cold weather waxing.)

Box F

Kick Waxing for Recreational Touring

1) Sand the base wax with #100 sandpaper to improve the bond between it and the kick wax you will use.

2) Apply the appropriate kick wax (Box E-2) by rubbing it onto the kick zone.

3) Cork or iron it in. Ironing is better.

4) Apply two or three additional layers and cork each into the ironed wax. Three or four thin layers are better than one thick layer, which is difficult to cork smooth. Leaving the wax rough does not improve the grip, but will reduce the glide. If you need a better grip, use a softer wax.

Box G

Kick Waxing for Racing

1) Clean the base. Coat with a soft hot wax (CH8 or CH10) and scrape immediately.

2) After the wax has cooled, brush away the excess wax with a hard bristle brush.

3) Choose the proper wax (see Box E), apply and iron. Let it cool. Ironing again in about 20 minutes will increase the durability of the wax.

4) If hard waxes (cold temperature) are used, scrape away the thick layer while the wax is still in a semisoft state.

5) Scrape the groove, the sidewalls and the edges. Clean the sidewalls with Fibertex™.

6) Scrape with a sharp flexible scraper (Swix 823).

7) Brush wax. For harder waxes use a mixed fiber brush (T155), softer waxes a stiff nylon brush (T161).

8) Scrape lightly with the Plexi Scraper.

9) Repeat step 7, then brush with a softer brush.

Box H

Kick Waxing for Colder Weather or New Snow

1) Choose the wax which you think will do the job. (You should have several waxes available — preferably from the same manufacturer.) If you are not sure of which wax to use, go with the harder wax first.

2) Wax at room temperature.

3) The colder the snow, the thinner the wax coat should be.

4) For harder snows and colder temperatures rub on the wax as if you were coloring the base with a crayon.

5) Polish in with a waxing cork or iron it on. To increase the life of the wax, it must be attached firmly to the base by heat or pressure.

6) If you are going on a long tour, use several layers of wax in the kick area.

7) If you need a better grip then a thicker coat is preferable to the multilayered technique.

For a better kick in warmer temperatures and/or on older snow, you will use a sticky, klister type wax. If the klister is not at room temperature, you may not be able to get it out of the tube. If this is the case, warm it in your hands or over the car radiator. If you haven't worked with klister, be careful. It can get all over your body, clothes, car and house. Squeeze the klister from the tube in a small bead on to the wax pocket area of the base. Spread a single bead of klister on each side of the groove, between the groove and the edge. Keep it out of the tracking groove in the middle of the base. If you are working inside, use a blow torch or iron to melt the klister along the ski. Some people like to use the heel of their hands to warm and spread the klister. It is messy, but effective. Spread the melted klister with a spreader along the wax pocket. You may need to torch it and spread it in small sections rather than doing the whole kick zone at a time. The finished coat should be about as thick as a coat of paint.

This method will give you a longer-wearing layer of klister. The alternative, which is quicker and can be used on the tour, is to use a klister spray and spread it with the accompanying sponge. Since this sprayed coat is thinner it won't last as long as the klister from the tube. (See Box I.)

Always clean the klister from the ski at the end of the tour. Use a nonflammable, nontoxic remover if possible.

Sticking and Slipping

As we said earlier, you seldom get an absolutely perfect wax job which is ideal for the whole run.

If you find yourself slipping, try a thicker coat of the same wax or a softer wax. If that doesn't work, check to see if the skis are too stiff so that the pressure

Box I

Kick Waxing with Klister for Warm Temperatures, Older Snow

1) Squeeze the klister from the tube in a small bead on to the wax pocket area of the base. Spread a single bead of klister on each side of the groove, between the groove and the edge. Keep it out of the tracking groove in the middle of the base.

2) Use a blow torch or iron to melt the klister along the ski. Some people like to use the heel of their hands to warm and spread the klister. It is messy but effective.

3) Spread the klister with a spreader along the wax pocket. You may need to torch it and spread to small sections at a time. The finished coat should be about as thick as a coat of paint. This method will give you a longer wearing layer of klister. The alternative, which is quicker and can be used on the tour, is to use a klister spray and spread it with the accompanying sponge. Since the coat is thinner, it won't last as long as the use of the klister from the tube.

4) Always clean the klister from the ski at the end of the tour. Use a nonflammable, nontoxic remover if possible.

of the pushoff does not bend the ski allowing the wax pocket to grip the snow. Possibly your technique is poor. You could be starting the kick too late or not pushing hard enough. Another possibility is that you put kick wax over glider wax. Kick wax usually won't adhere to the harder wax. (See Box J.)

If you find yourself sticking in the snow or have a poor glide, the wax pocket may be too long so that the kick wax slows your glide. Another possibility is that the gliding sections of your skis may need glide waxing. Your glide wax should be in the areas which touch the snow when your weight is evenly distributed on both skis. Often the bottom of the skis have picked up ice. If this is the case, scrape them fully and be sure to keep them in the snow when you ski. Lifting your skis will increase the chance of water freezing on the bottoms. (See Box K.)

Box J

Correcting Problems of Backslip (Poor Grip)

1) Try a thicker coat of the same wax or a softer wax.

2) Are the skis too stiff so that the pressure of the pushoff does not bend the ski so that the wax pocket reaches the snow?

3) Is the technique poor — starting the kick too late or not pushing hard enough?

4) Did you put kick wax over glider wax? It usually won't adhere to the harder wax.

Box K
Correcting Problems of Stickiness (Insufficient Glide)

1) The wax pocket may be too long so that the kick wax slows your glide.

2) The gliding sections of the skis may need glide waxing. Your glide wax will be in the areas which touch the snow when your weight is evenly distributed on both skis.

3) The bottom of the skis may have picked up ice. Scrape them fully and keep them in the snow when you ski. Lifting your skis will increase the chance of water freezing on the bottoms.

Box L
Classic Ski Waxing for the Glide Zones

1) If you want to wax the gliding sections of the ski, melt paraffin wax and paint or iron it on the gliding sections of the ski — the front and the tail. Let it stand for a half hour to set.

2) Use a plastic scraper to peel off most of the wax — leaving only a thin coat. Always move the scraper up and down the ski, never across its narrow width.

3) Remove the paraffin from the tracking groove with the rounded section of the scraper.

4) Iron the wax into the ski and brush it. Or use an FC 100 (for -15 to 0 C, 5 to 32 F) or FC 200 (for -4 to +15 C, 25 to 60 F) or refer to the gliding chart for racers (Box E 1) to get the best type of gliding wax for the conditions.

5) Brush with the proper brush to remove wax from the rills.

To improve your glide as a classic (diagonal stride) skier, you will want to wax the tip and tail areas — up to the wax pocket. Melt paraffin wax and paint or iron it on the gliding sections of the ski — the front and the tail. Let it stand for a half hour to set. Then use a plastic scraper to peel off most of the wax — leaving only a thin coat. Always move the scraper up and down the ski, never across its narrow width. Remove the paraffin from the tracking groove with the rounded section of the scraper. Rub the paraffin into the ski with a waxing cork. If you want a more effective and more expensive gliding wax, refer to the gliding chart for racers to get the best type of gliding wax for the conditions. (See Box L for waxing technique, Box E-1 for gliding waxes.)

Gliding Waxes for Skaters

Skaters use glide wax over the whole ski because their power comes from the inside edge of the skating ski. They therefore don't need kick wax. So for skating just put glide wax over the whole ski base. Not much of a trick to that, is there? Well, maybe, because there are a number of different glide waxes. The Swix Cera Nova series is considered to be the best system in the world. In order to develop this system of 14 different waxes, a large amount of research was required. About 80 percent of the top ski racers in the world use the Swix Cera Nova system for glide waxing.

Often, particularly for races, manmade snow is used with natural snow. For this colder manmade snow, higher amounts of hard, brittle, synthetic paraffins are used. If the snow is warmer, less synthetic wax is used, but more fluorocarbon additives are added.

You can melt some wax on an old electric iron, then iron the wax on the ski. Then you scrape it off with a plastic scraper and use a cork to rub it in. You can also melt the wax in a pan and paint on a thin coat, then iron it. Always finish with brushing to make certain that the rills are able to remove the water under the base effectively.

Gliding Waxes for the Recreational Skier

The recreational skier may use only one of two gliding waxes: Swix FC 100 if it is colder (5 to 32 degrees F, -15 to 0 C) or FC 200 if it is warmer. If these waxes are too expensive for your taste, use the CH (hydrocarbon) type of wax. Rub on the wax, then using a cork, rub it in, and smooth it or iron it on. If you iron it on, you can cork it, or scrape it and brush it, then scrape with a sharp flexible scraper (Swix 823). Brush the wax. For harder waxes use a mixed fiber brush (T155); for softer waxes a stiff nylon brush (T161). (See Box M.)

Box M

Waxing for a Recreational Skating Tour

1) Clean the base.

2) Choose the proper wax or waxes (See Box E-1). Skaters will use a glide wax the whole length of the ski.

3) The recreational skier may use the less expensive CH (hydrocarbon) or the more expensive Swix FC 100 if it is colder (if temperature is between -15 to 0 C, +5 to +32 F) or FC 200 if it is warmer (if temperature is between -4 and +15 C, 25 to 60 F).

4) Rub on the wax, then using a cork, rub it in and smooth it on — or iron it on. If you iron it on, you can either cork it in or scrape it and brush it.

   • If you scrape, use a sharp flexible scraper (Swix 823), then brush the wax. For harder waxes use a mixed fiber brush (T155), for softer waxes a stiff nylon brush (T161).

5) Brush with a properly stiff brush to remove wax from the rills.

Gliding Waxes for Racing

If you are waxing for racing, clean the base with a solvent or with hot wax. Apply a coat of soft hot wax (CH8 or CH10) and scrape immediately. Let the wax cool, then brush away the excess wax with a hard bristle brush. Select the proper wax (See chart in Box E-1), apply it and iron it in. Let it cool. Iron it again in about 20 minutes. This will increase the durability of the wax. If hard waxes, particularly the FC waxes, are used, scrape away the thick layer while the wax is still in a semisoft state. Be sure to scrape the groove, the sidewalls and the edges, and clean the sidewalls with Fibertex™.

Scrape with a sharp flexible scraper (Swix 823), then brush the wax. For harder waxes, use a mixed fiber brush (T155); for softer waxes, a stiff nylon brush (T161). Then scrape lightly with the Plexi Scraper. Repeat the process then brush with a softer brush. (See Box N.)

Box N

Waxing for Skating (Free Style) Races

1) Clean the base with a solvent or with hot wax. To clean with hot wax: Apply a coat of soft, hot wax (CH8 or CII10) and scrape immediately. Let the wax cool, then brush away the excess wax with a hard bristle brush.

2) Select the proper wax (see chart in Box E-1), apply it and iron it in. Let it cool, then iron it again in about 20 minutes. This will increase the durability of the wax.

   • If hard waxes, particularly the FC waxes, are used, scrape away the thick layer while the wax is still in a semisoft state. Be sure to scrape the groove, the sidewalls and the edges, and clean the sidewalls with Fibertex™.

3) Scrape with a sharp flexible scraper (Swix 823), then brush the wax.

   • For harder waxes use a mixed fiber brush (T155).

   • For softer waxes use a stiff nylon brush (T161).

4) Scrape lightly with the Plexi Scraper.

5) Repeat the process then brush with a softer brush.

Box O

Be Prepared on the Trail

Take along:

1) at least one harder and one softer wax, possibly more.

2) a small piece of towel for drying the ski if it must be rewaxed.

3) a scraper and cork.

Box P
Troubleshooting

1) If you are not getting proper glide the gliding area is probably not sufficiently scraped, so scrape off the wax in the gliding area and brush it out.

2) If your ski is a bit too slippery, the kick zone wax may be too thin, so apply more wax or the problem may be with the track in which you are skiing; if so, apply more kick wax to the front of the kick zone and extend the kick zone forward.

3) If your ski is very slippery, you probably used the wrong wax, a wax for a colder temperature, so scrape off the wax and apply a softer wax; or the temperature may be quickly warming; again, apply a softer wax.

4) If your ski does not glide well, the wax may be too thick, so thin it with a scraper and rebrush it; or your wax may be too soft, so scrape the wax and apply a harder wax over the base wax.

5) If your ski ices up (ice on the bottom):

   • The ski may have been too warm when you put it on the snow. If so, scrape the ice off, brush the base, and let the ski cool.

   • The wax job may not cover the entire area needed or it may be too thick in some areas. If so, remove the ice, smooth the wax and brush it.

   • You may have been standing too much and not skiing when the snow is at about 0 degrees Celsius (32 Fahrenheit). If so move the skis forward and back to scrape off the ice.

6) If your ski drags and patches of snow are formed under the ski base, the wax layer is too soft or too thick. Remove the wax with a scraper and, if needed, apply a harder wax.

STEP BY STEP
New Cross Country Skis

Preparation should take place indoors, at room temperature. A stable support is required.

If the skis are finished by stone grinding, start with Step 4.

1 Adjustment and alignment of the base finish with Swix Sandpaper Grit #100. Slightly round off the side edges with the same paper.

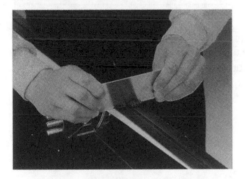

2 Remove all polyethylene microburrs with the Swix Steel Scraper T80.

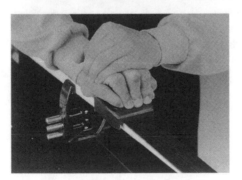

3 Apply a new structure with the Swix Super Riller T401 with the standard 0.75mm cutting blade.

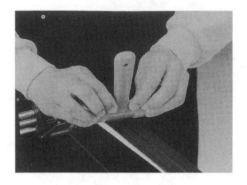

4 Lightly level off the peaks of the structure with the steel scraper of Swix Razorblade Scraper T89.

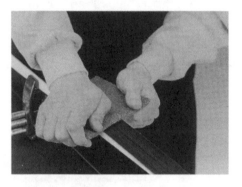

5 Use Fibertex 265 to deburr any remaining micro-burrs and to round off any sharp edges to the structure rills.

6 Define the kick zone on classical skis.
Sand the kick wax zone lengthwise with #100 grit paper.

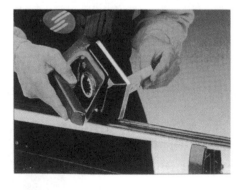

7 Saturate the base by ironing on a soft, pene-trating wax such as CH10 with the Swix Waxing Iron T7311/7322.

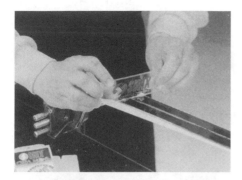

8 Scrape the wax while it is still hot from ironing using the Plexi Scraper and Groove Scraper.

Repeat the wax application. Allow cooling before scraping. Repeat at least three times.

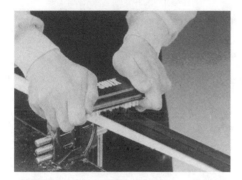

9 Any remaining wax should be brushed off with the White Nylon Brush T161, and preferably also with the Mixed Fiber Brush T155.

10 Repeat using Fibertex 266 and the Razorblade Scraper T89 to cut more of the remaining microfibers.

11 Apply the wax suitable for day's conditions.

STEP BY STEP
Racing Skis

Preparation should take place indoors at room temperature.

A stable support is required.

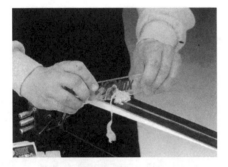

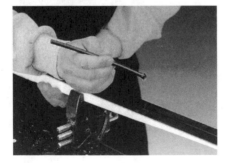

1 STEP BY STEP PREPARATION - GLIDE ZONE
This is a general description used by top level technicians.

Scrape off the travel wax using a Plexi Scraper and Groove Scraper.

2 Brush with the White Nylon Brush T161. Follow with the mixed Fiber Brush T155.

3 Repair the base melting the Polystick T170 or T171 into any damaged spots.

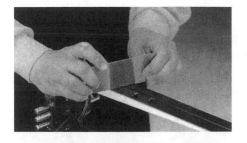

4 Remove excess polyethylene material from the repair after cooling with the Steel Scraper T80 or Body File T108. Finish by sanding the repaired area with #220 sandpaper.

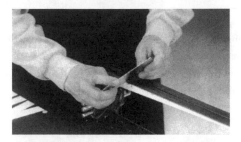

5 Smooth the side edges with the Steel Scraper T80 and/or sandpaper #180.

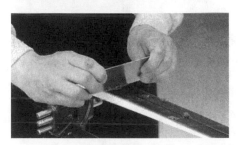

6 If necessary further adjustment and alignment of the base should be done with the Steel Scraper and/or Swix sandpaper.

7 If any new structuring is required use the Super Riller T401 with the appropriate rilling steel.

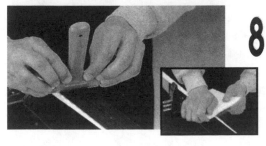

8 Make some light strokes along the base with the Razorblade Scraper to cut the peaks off the structure rills. Also use Fibertex T266 to slightly round off any sharp edges from the structure. This Fibertex treatment also removes base oxidation.

9 Clean the base with wax using the "Hot Scrape" method with a soft wax such as CH8 or CH10.

10 After cooling brush away any remaining wax using the White Nylon Brush and The Mixed Fiber Brush T155.

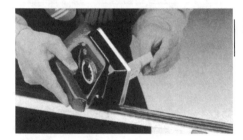

11 Apply the race wax to fit the conditions based upon the Cera Nova Waxing Chart.

12 Carefully iron the wax. Repeated ironing after 20 minutes of cooling will increase the wax duration in the base.

13 If cold temperature waxes are used, scrape the thick layer away while the wax is still in a semi-soft state.

14 Scrape the groove, sidewalls, and edges.

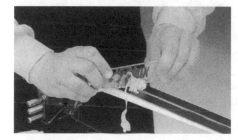

15 Clean the sidewalls with Fibertex T266.
Apply F4, let dry, and polish.

16 Scrape the base with a sharp Plexi Scraper T823.

17 Brush with the White nylon Brush T161.
For harder waxes use the Mixed Fiber Brush
T155.

18 Make some more light passes with the Plexi
Scraper.

19 Continue brushing with the White Nylon Brush T161 and/or the Mixed Fiber Brush T155 for finer structures/colder waxes.

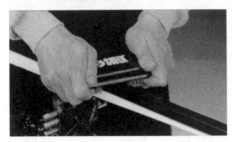

20 Final brushing is done with the Blue Nylon Brush T160.

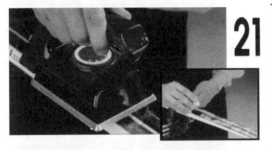

21 **FOR CERA F CONDITIONS FOLLOW THESE STEPS:**

Apply Cera F. Distribute the powder evenly on the base. Iron the Cera F. Sufficient temperature is reached to bond Cera F to the base when small sparkling "stars" dance on the base just behind the iron.

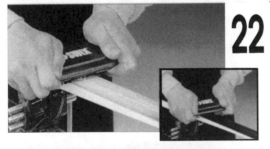

22 Brush the Cera F thoroughly after cooling with the Horsehair Brush T157. Finish with the Blue Nylon Brush T160.

NOTE: All the brushing steps can be done with the corresponding Roto Brush for faster completion.

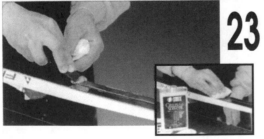

23 **AFTER THE RACE**

Clean the kick zone from hardwax or klister. Use the groove scraper and clean any remaining wax with Swix Fiberlene T150 and Swix Wax Remover I74.

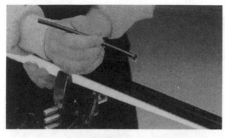

24 Inspect the base for damage and make necessary repairs.

25 Clean the glide zones with the Mixed Fiber Brush T155. If the bases are exceptionally dirty use Swix Wax Remover I74 before brushing.

26 Make a few passes with Fibertex T266 to remove oxidation.

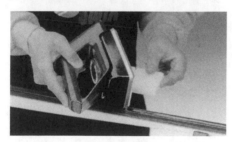

27 Protect the base by ironing on a layer of a soft, penetrating wax such as CH8 or CH10.

28 Strap the skis together with the Swix Ski Strap R400 or R395.

11

Conditioning

Skiing requires several different types of conditioning. You will need endurance training to make your cardiorespiratory (heart-lung-blood) system work efficiently. You also will need endurance in the individual muscles, particularly the abdominals, the upper back, arms and thighs. You will need strength to push yourself with your poles, to push off on your power stride and to hold your body in a tuck when going down hill. And you should have a certain amount of flexibility in your joints so that you can easily go through a full range of motion. Agility and balance are also important to be able to have all of your weight on one ski while gliding.

Conditioning for Endurance

Cross country skiers have been shown to be the best conditioned athletes in terms of cardiopulmonary endurance. The sport is therefore an ideal activity for those who want to feel fit, extend their lives, reduce heart disease and cancer risks, control their weight and generally feel better. The benefits, of course, depend on how well trained the skier is. For someone who skis a half hour or more a day, the benefits are very good.

If you can ski every day — great! If not, you should look to other forms of endurance exercise, such as running, swimming or cycling to maintain aerobic fitness. Upon reaching the aerobic level, several changes begin to occur. More red blood cells are activated. These cells carry oxygen from the lungs to the muscles; then on the way back to the lungs, they carry carbon dioxide from the muscles to the lungs. While much of the blood is already circulating, under the demands of exercise more blood from other organs can flow into the circulatory system. The liver and spleen are particularly important in this action.

After exercising, many of these red cells remain in circulation. In a few days, however, a large number will go back to storage in the organs. But daily endurance exercise will keep most of the red cells circulating. Your body will then recognize that it needs more red cells so it will create more — if you have sufficient protein, iron, copper, vitamin B$_{12}$ and the other ingredients necessary to manufacture the cells.

You benefit in several ways. Your body will recover more quickly following your tour, and you will be less fatigued. And since your total blood volume has increased, your body will be cleansed more quickly from all the toxic wastes which tend to build within us, even if we are active.

If a doctor were to take a red blood cell count before you began an exercise program, then take another sample after you had exercised effectively for an hour, you would find that your red cell count had increased. Since you have more red cells circulating in your blood, each teaspoon of blood will be able to carry more oxygen to the muscles and more carbon dioxide away from them.

Very simply stated this is how you provide fuel to your muscles:

■ Oxygen which you breathe is attracted to the blood cells by the hemoglobin.

■ Simple sugars, the simplest usable form of the food you have consumed, are added to the blood.

■ From the atoms in these substances, the body's own energy sources are re-built.

■ What remains is carbon dioxide and water. The carbon dioxide is then exhaled.

Obviously, the more red cells you have the more efficiently you can transport oxygen to the muscles and carbon dioxide away from them. This becomes even more important when you move to higher altitudes. At sea level, nearly 21 percent of air is oxygen. Almost 79 percent is nitrogen. When you exhale, almost 16 percent of your exhaled air is oxygen and about 3½ percent is carbon dioxide.

If you were go to an altitude of 10,000 feet (3,050 meters), the amount of available oxygen drops about 30 percent. To make up for this lack of oxygen, you will breathe more often as you become acclimated to the altitude. In about a week, your red blood cells will have increased. Still, the amount of oxygen in your blood will have dropped by about 8 percent. When you come back to a lower altitude, you will have more endurance for several days because the increased number of red cells will stay with you for a while. This is why endurance athletes such as cross country skiers, marathon runners and swimmers often train at higher altitudes.

If you have trained effectively aerobically at the lower elevations by doing aerobic dance, running, swimming, cycling or long-distance skating, your red cells will have already increased, and you will be more ready for exercise at the higher elevation.

To improve your endurance, you must increase your heart rate significantly for at least 20 to 30 minutes. This is long enough to give you the necessary benefits to reduce heart attack risk. But if you are training for a two-, three- or four-hour ski tour, you will benefit by longer workouts.

How much cardiorespiratory fitness you need is dependent on how and where you will ski. If you can walk out of your front door and put on your skis and merely want a leisurely glide though the woods, forget this program and just lace up your boots whenever you are ready. But if you want to go on a long or a fast tour, or you are going to a much higher altitude to ski, you are well advised to begin a conditioning program before your trip.

It is wise to work out at least three days a week — six is better — for six weeks. But, of course, anything is better than nothing.

As you probably know, the generally accepted standard for endurance exercise is to get your heart rate to an acceptable level for 20 to 30 minutes. That "acceptable" level is 60 to 85 percent of your maximum heart rate. And your maximum heart rate is considered to be 220 heartbeats per minute less your age. So if you are 20 years old it would be 220 minus 20 which is 200. You then work out with a pulse rate of between 130 and 170 for 20 to 30 minutes. If you are 40 years old, the calculations would be 220 - 40 = 180, so you would work out with a pulse rate of between 117 and 153. If you are 60 the figures would be 220 - 60 = 160, so your target heart rate would be between 104 and 136. The higher number (the 85 percent level) is more desirable because your body will be working harder.

If you are in average condition, your resting pulse rate will be in the 70s. As you get in better shape, your resting pulse rate will drop because you will have more red blood cells working for you so your heart doesn't have to beat as often to get its work done. You can tell if you are getting in better condition by measuring your resting pulse rate. When it drops into the mid-60s, you are in better than average condition. When it gets into the 50s you are in pretty good shape. In the 40s you are in great shape. A few world class endurance athletes have pulse rates in the 20s.

To check your pulse you can put your fingers, not the thumb, on the opposite wrist just above the thumb. Or you can put them just below your ear on the inside of the muscle on the side of your neck. Some people just like to put their hands over their hearts and feel the beat. Once you get the beat, count the number of beats in a minute. This is your pulse rate. Or you can count for 15 seconds and multiply that number by 4 to get the number of beats in a minute. If you are exercising, it is often easiest to count the beats for only 6 seconds then multiply that number by 10 to get your pulse rate during exercise.

Before you start an exercise program, it is always a good idea to have a physical examination. This will give you your blood pressure, your cholesterol levels, your red blood cell count, the condition of your heart and a number of other important indicators.

Any exercise that gets your heart beating fast enough to get into your target zone is good. Cross country skiing, swimming, running, cycling — even sex. Just remember that whatever you are doing, get to your target rate and stay there for at least 20 minutes. Thirty is better. Also you should warm up before you hit your target range. So just perform your activity at a little slower pace for a few minutes before you speed up and hit your target rate. Then at the end of your exercise, cool down by slowing your exercise and letting your heart rate drop. Then finish with some stretching. Some people like to stretch before their aerobic workout. That's OK. Just do some aerobic warm-up, such as jogging or skiing; stretch; get into your real aerobic workout; then stretch again. The stretching after the workout is more important than that done before the workout.

Developing Muscular Endurance

It's not enough to have a healthy heart and lots of red blood cells. Individual muscles also have to have specific endurance. Muscles used in an endurance activity will develop a better capacity to use the oxygen and sugars which the blood brings to them. There will be more hemoglobin in the muscles, more readily available fuel, and there may even be a different type of muscle tissue developed.

There are three different types of muscle fibers, the slow-twitch (red or type I), the intermediate (type II a), and the fast-twitch (white or type II b). The fast-twitch fibers contract quickly, but cannot endure many repetitions. Olympic weight lifters have a high percentage of these because they need only one powerful contraction, then they rest for many minutes. Endurance athletes, such as cross country skiers, swimmers and distance runners have a large percentage of the slow-twitch fibers. These fibers contain more fuel and can contract many times.

Research indicates that the type of training a person does can change the type of fibers present. It may be that it is the intermediate fibers which change more toward the fast- or the slow-twitch (type II) of fiber. Trained cross country skiers have 70 to 80% of their muscle fibers as the slow twitch (type II) variety. Marathon runners are more likely to be over 80 percent. It would seem then that appropriate aerobic training should result in more effective muscles and better muscular endurance.

In the off-season, the summer and fall, swimming (especially the crawl or the back stroke) will not only help to maintain your aerobic level in the cardiorespiratory system, but it will develop more of the slow-twitch fibers in the upper back (latissimus dorsi) and the back of the arms (triceps). This development should help your arms for poling next season. On the other hand, skating, running or cycling should help to develop muscles in the legs.

For these reasons, many people do "cross training" in the off-season. This may include two or three days of running, cycling, skating or working on a cross country ski machine (such as NordicTrack) for the lower body and two or three days of swimming, rowing or paddling for the upper body.

Another exercise, which will condition your legs, can be done while you watch TV. Put five or six books on the floor in a stack. Start with both feet on one side of the books then jump to the other side, landing on both feet. Continue to jump back and forth without stopping until next December or until the first snow falls. Boy, will you be in great shape for the season! Jumping rope is another exercise which will condition both your heart and your legs.

Increasing Your Strength

Muscular endurance and muscular strength are at opposite ends of the spectrum. Strength is how much force you can generate in one muscular contraction, while endurance is how long you can continue muscular contractions with relatively little resistance against them.

In Nordic skiing you never need the maximum force that an Olympic weight lifter would need. But there are times when you need more than the normal amount of force, such as when going up a hill or even when getting up after a fall.

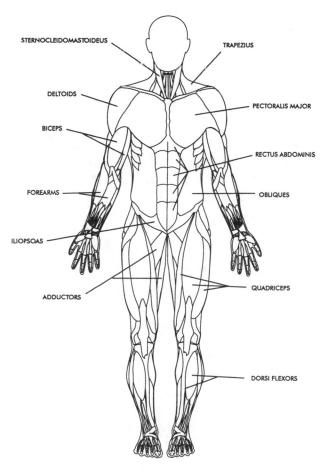

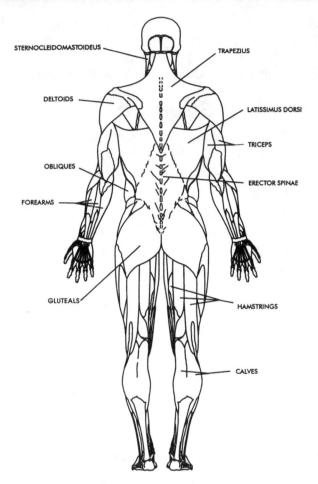

Your strength is determined primarily by the number of individual muscle fibers you have contracting in one contraction. No one can contract all of the muscle fibers in a muscle at the same time. Few people can even contract 50 percent of their muscle fibers at one time. So your strength training program is designed to teach your brain to be able to contract more muscle fibers at one time. Strength can greatly increase the force exerted by your power ski and by your poling action. This, in turn, will increase your glide and your stride distance.

The following exercises will help you to condition your muscles. If you are trying to get stronger, exhaust your muscles in less than 10 repetitions. Exhaustion in one to three repetitions is best. But if you are working on developing muscular endurance, such as you will use in cross country skiing, do a number of repetitions. A good range for most people would be 25 to 100. But remember that your muscles should be exhausted when you finish. You know you're exhausted when you can no longer eke out one more repetition. It is only by getting your muscles very tired that will get you the best results. However, keep in mind that anything is better than nothing.

Strength Exercises for the Abdomen

The Abdominal Curl: Everyone knows this exercise but some have not kept up with the latest techniques to make it more effective. Lie on the floor or on your bed:

1) Put your hands on your chest (to avoid pulling in on the neck muscles).

2) Bring your feet up as close to your hips as possible (so that you don't use the small hip flexing muscles which attach to the lower back — especially important for women).

3) Look at the ceiling and continue looking at the same spot during the exercise (so that you don't stretch the muscles in the back of your neck).

4) Raise your shoulders and concentrate on bringing the lower part of your ribs closer to the top of your hips.

5) Do as many repetitions as you can because you want muscular endurance from these muscles.

This exercise strengthens the abdominal muscles which will begin your poling action. As you start to pole, you will use these muscles as you bend forward at the waist.

There are actually four sets of muscles in the abdominal wall. One, the rectus abdominis, does most of the work in the curl or sit-up. There are two sets of angled muscles called the obliques. These assist in the sit-up but also work in twisting and side bending actions. The following exercises work the obliques.

The Twisting Abdominal Curl is the same as the above exercise, but as you raise your shoulders you bring your right shoulder toward your left knee on one repetition, then your left shoulder to your right knee on the next one.

Curl Up

Twisting Curl Up

If you belong to a gym, there may be a rotary abdominal machine which is more effective than the twisting sit-up. Or you can work with a partner. While sitting in a chair holding a rod (broom, pipe, etc.) across your upper chest, have your partner give resistance to one end of the rod while you twist against it.

Sitting Trunk Twist

Another exercise which can develop the abdominal obliques is the side sit-up. Put your feet under a sofa or have someone hold them down; then, while on your side bring your shoulders and torso upward.

Side Sit-up

You can also do leg-overs. While lying on your back, raise your legs so that they are straight over your hips. Move them slowly to the right until they touch the floor then lift them back to the original position. Then repeat to the left.

Leg-overs

Strength Exercises for the Shoulders and Arms

Shoulder Extension is the most important exercise for cross country skiers to do unless they have been swimmers or gymnasts. The upper back, latissimus dorsi, and back of the arm muscles, triceps, are not used as often in other sports, but contribute much of the power to the poles.

If you belong to a gym use a pull-down pulley, and pull it down with your arms straight.

If you don't belong to a gym, you can buy stretching bands at a sporting goods store or surgical tubing (about 8 to 10 feet) from a pharmacy. Screw an eye bolt into a door jamb or into a wall in the garage; anchor the middle of the band to the bolt. Tie knots in the end of the tubes, or make a handle, then pull — alternating arms or using both arms together. You want to use your muscles through the same range of movement you will use in skiing, so pull from a spot directly in front of your shoulders to as far back as you can pull.

Using dumbbells, you can bend forward at the waist, then alternately bring your right arm as far back as you can, then do the same with the left arm. You can also lie on your back with your arms on the floor behind your head. With dumbbells, bricks or books, bring your arms forward until they are vertical over your head.

Shoulder Extensions – Lateral Pull-downs

Shoulder Extensions – Dumbells

Another way to develop these muscles is with a partner. Take two lengths of rope or two poles at least six feet long. Face each other. Each holds one end of each pole and pulls back with his or her right arm while resisting each other with the left arms. Then both pull with their left arms while they resist each other with their right arms. The pull and the resisting are working the lats and one of the three heads of the triceps. While doing this exercise keep the arms straight — no bend at the elbows.

Shoulder Extensions — Two Poles

The triceps (three heads) straighten (extend) the elbow. One of the three heads crosses the shoulder joint so it works with the lats in pulling the upper arm backwards. All three heads work to straighten the arm at the elbow joint. This is done in the last part of the poling action.

Tricep Extensions — Machine

Tricep Extensions — Dumbells

If you belong to a gym, use the triceps extension machine or do triceps extensions on the lat pull-down machine. You can also lift dumbbells over your

Push-ups

Knee Push-ups

head. If you don't belong to a gym, you can do push-ups with either your feet or your knees on the floor.

Strength Exercises for the Legs, Hips and Knees

The front of the thigh or quadriceps hold you in a tuck position when you are gliding on one leg, and they bring your legs forward as they recover from the push or "kick."

If you are in a gym, use the quadriceps machine. If not, get a partner. Sit on a table and have your partner place both hands on your ankle and give resistance. Straighten your leg. If you don't have a partner, you can use that same rubber band which was recommended for the upper back.

Quadriceps — Machine

Quadriceps — Manual

The back of the thigh or hamstrings provide most of the push backward on the ski. Gyms have special machines for the hamstrings. If you don't have access to a machine, get your trusty old partner, lie face down on the floor or a

Hamstrings —Machine

Hamstrings – Manual

table, and have your partner push against your ankle as you lift your lower leg from the floor. Keep your knee on the floor or table.

To get the upper part of the rear of the hips, the muscles that do most of the pushing work in your skiing, lie on a table face down with your hips on the table with your thighs past the table and your toes touching the floor. You can use a partner if you want more strength, or do it alone if you want more endurance by doing many repetitions. Start with one toe touching the floor while the other leg is brought as high as possible, then alternate legs. This will look like an exaggerated kicking action for a person swimming the crawl stroke. Another partner exercise for hip extension is mentioned under the hip flexion exercise.

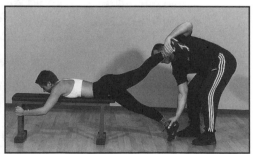

Hip Extensions on Table with Partner

Hip and knee extension give greater force potential from your hips and knees. Gyms all have either squat racks or other machines which allow you to extend your legs. But it can be done easily at home. You can just do a three-quarter knee bend (don't bend your knees more than 90 degrees), or you can do half knee bends if you want twice the amount of resistance. To do a half knee bend, hold a table top to steady yourself. Using only one leg, bend down 45 to 90 degrees then return to a standing position. By doing it on only one leg, you get the same effect as doing it with two legs while holding a barbell equal to your own weight.

Hip and Knee Extensions — Sled

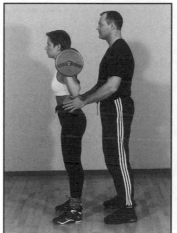

Hip and Knee Extensions — Squat

Hip and Knee Extensions — One Legged Squat

Hip Extensions on Multihip Machine

Calf — One Leg Rise

Calf muscles (gastrocnemius) are strengthened by simply rising up on your toes then bringing your heels back to the ground. Repeat many times for endurance. If you want more strength, such as for hill climbing, balance yourself by holding a table or chair then do the exercise using only one leg at a time — the right leg until it is exhausted, then the left leg until it is exhausted.

Hip abductors move your legs sideways away from the midline of your body. They are very important in helping you to maintain balance. When shifting your weight to the new gliding ski, it is the abductors, those muscles on the outside of your lower hip, which stop your motion outward and allow you to catch your balance. They are also involved in the pushing action of a skater.

Hip Abductors — Multihip Machine

Some gyms have special machines for the abductors. If there is a "multi-hip" machine, use it. Most gyms have low pulley weights with ankle straps. Stand with one side of your body next to the machine, and put the ankle strap on the leg farthest from the machine. Lift the leg sideways keeping it straight.

With a partner, lie on your side. Let your partner put pressure on your knee or ankle, then lift your leg as high as you can. If you have no partner, you can do the same exercise alone — you just won't get as strong, but you can get just as much endurance. You can also do it yourself by sitting with your knees

Hip Abductors — Alone

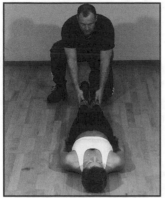

Hip Abductors — With Partner

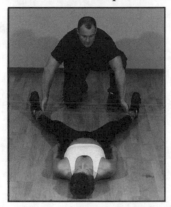

Hip Adductors — With Partner

close to your chest, then give pressure with your hands to the outside of your knees as you bring your knees outward.

You can also use the rubber bands. Attach one to a low part of a wall, hook your foot into a loop on the end of the band and lift your leg outward.

Hip adductors are those muscles high on the inside of your thighs. They bring your legs back together if they have been moved outward by the abductors. The exercises are just the reverse of those for the abductors.

If your gym has a machine, use it. If there is a low pulley station, stand sideways to the pulley but a yard away from the machine. Put the strap on the ankle nearest the machine. Let your leg move outward (toward the machine) with the weight, then bring it back to the other leg.

Hip Adductors — Alone

With a partner lie on your back. Spread your legs. Let your partner give pressure inside your ankles. Bring your legs back together. If you wish, you can combine the adductor and abductor muscles in this exercise. While lying on your back, your partner will give you hand pressure on the outside of both ankles. You will spread your legs against the pressure (abductors). Then your partner will give you pressure on the inside of your ankles, and you will bring your legs back together (adductors).

Without a partner just sit on the floor with your feet about 12 inches from your hips and the heels together. Spread your knees outward, then grasp the inside of your knees with your hands. Bring your knees together as you resist the movement with your hands. You will feel the tension inside your upper thighs.

Hip Flexion — Multihip Machine

Hip flexion exercises help you to quickly bring the ski forward after the power phase. It can be done on a multi-hip machine or with a partner. If you have a partner you can lie on your right side. With your left leg back, as if you have just finished a long stride, have your partner put pressure on the front of your ankle, then bring your leg as far forward as you can. The farther forward you go the less power you will have, so your partner will need to apply less pressure as you move your leg forward.

Thigh Rotation

Once the leg is forward, your partner can put pressure on the back of your heel, then you can swing your leg back as far as it will go. This is hip extension.

Thigh rotation develops the muscles which move your ski tips in or out. This action is done high in the hips. Sit on the floor with your legs stretched out. Turn your feet inward as far as they can go and hold. Then twist outward — and hold. It is more effective if a partner can give your feet resistance in each direction.

Exercises for the Lower Back

Lower back exercises should be geared to muscular endurance more than strength, so you will want many repetitions. You can lie on the floor face down and lift your shoulders about six inches from the floor then return to the floor. (You don't want to go too high with your shoulders because you don't want to create a "sway back" in your exercise.)

You can also do this with a partner. With the partner holding your legs, and your hips and legs on a table, bend forward at the waist to 60 or 90 degrees then lift your torso back up so that it is in line with your legs and hips. Again, you don't want to arch your back during the exercise.

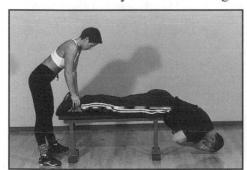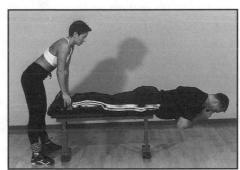

Lower Back — Table Exercise with Partner

Repetitions and Weight

How many reps and how much weight you use depends on your goals. For pure strength, you should be exhausted in one to three repetitions. But pure strength is not what you want for skiing. You want a certain amount of strength and you want muscular endurance. Aim for between 20 to more than 100 repetitions. You may have to work up to 20 reps from just a few reps. Don't be discouraged. Anything you do will help.

Using "manual resistance" with a partner can actually be better than using weights. Your partner can adjust the pressure to make you work to a maximum level on each repetition. Weights can't do this. Only partners and "isokinetic" machines have this capability. So if you are using a partner, don't figure you are not getting the best strength workout. In fact, that partner is probably entitled to a good dinner once a week for helping you to develop your "habit."

If you are a racer and one group of muscles needs more conditioning, a reverse pyramid workout is suggested. For this you will need a weight machine.

Start at the level where you can do only one repetition. Do it. Try another. Then decrease the weight and repeat the exercise. Continue this, exercising to exhaustion at every step, until you have done a total of 200 repetitions. This is only for the highly dedicated racer and should only be done for one or two muscle groups at each workout.

Becoming More Flexible

Flexibility comes from stretching the body's connective tissue — the tissue that holds one bone to another (ligaments), the tissue which holds muscles to bones (tendons) and the tissue which holds the individual muscle bundles together. If you are not flexible, you will not have a full range of motion for each joint. When you are too tight, you must use excess muscle power just to make a simple movement.

For example, if the connective tissue in the front of your hips is too tight, you won't be able to extend your ski as far backward in your power stroke. If the connective tissue in the front of the shoulders is too tight you won't be able to push back as far with your poles. Also, if you are not sufficiently flexible, it is easier to sprain (ligament damage) or strain (muscular or tendon damage).

Flexibility is quite simple to achieve. Most of us touched our toes every day during physical education classes in school, but we may have forgotten to continue the practice. You could probably easily touch your toes when you were 12. Can you do it now? The connective tissue tends to shorten if we do not keep it stretched, so most of us have lost some flexibility between the time we were in the eighth grade and now. So we need to get back into some of our childhood habits.

Stretches should be held for 20 to 30 seconds in order to get the maximum benefits. If you find that you are particularly tight in one area, do the exercise several times a day.

Toe Touch

Leg Straddle

The Toe Touch keeps your lower back and the back of your hips and thighs flexible. While most people do it standing, it is more effective to do it sitting on the floor. When you are sitting and stretching forward, the muscles in the back of your torso and thighs relax so you can stretch farther. When you are standing,

Splits

those same muscles remain somewhat tight because they are fighting the gravity which is allowing you to bend downward.

The leg straddle stretches the tissue of the upper inner thighs. This allows you to spread your legs more easily in a sideways movement such as when doing the wedge or skating. While standing, move your feet sideways wiggling them farther and farther out each day.

The splits are a forward-backward stretch for the tissue at the front and the rear of the upper thighs. Becoming flexible in these areas makes it easier to do any striding or skating and allows an effortless reach for the glide. Put the right foot forward and the left back. Keep moving them farther and farther apart. Then put the left leg forward and the right back.

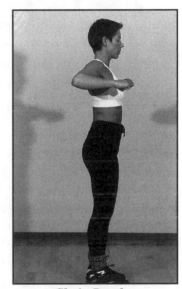

Chain Breaker

Standing Trunk Twist

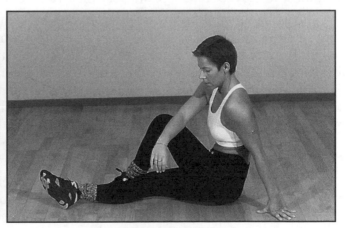

Sitting Trunk Twist

147

The upper chest and shoulder stretch (chain breaker) is not only good to prevent round shoulders, but it will also allow you to use a longer poling action. With your arms at shoulder level, pull them backwards as far as they will go — and hold.

Trunk twists stretch the middle of your torso. You will want to be flexible in this area, especially for classic skiing. You can stretch from the sitting position or the standing position.

The front of the shoulder stretch also allows you to push farther back with your arms in the poling action. While standing with your arms at your side, bring both arms directly backward as far as you can — and hold.

Training for Agility and Balance

You are already well aware that skiing is a balance sport along with its endurance requirements. Skiing technique is all about balance in motion. Just think about all of the internal and external factors that must be balanced and counterbalanced to skate and glide or to ski down a difficult run. You've got the steepness of the slope, the depth and density of the snow, the texture of the snow and the visibility, all of which vary from turn to turn. In order to skillfully ski through all this, you've got to be balanced on one ski most of the time. When turning you must guide them left and right in order to regulate your speed and momentum. Indeed, high-level skiing requires an unbelievable sense of balance and equilibrium.

You cannot get enough work on balance, on or off the snow. When you balance you are training your brain. It must continually make adjustments in your muscle contractions to keep you from falling right or left, forward or backward. If you are standing on one leg, your balance forward and backward is easy to find, because your foot is longer than it is wide so your forward-backward balance is easier than your side-to-side balance. If you put on skis, this difference is emphasized because the ski is longer than your foot and also narrower than most feet. And it is more slippery than your foot bottoms.

So while forward-backward balance is essential, it is much easier to achieve than side-to-side balance. Add to this the fact that while skiing, you shift your weight from one ski to the other quickly. If you are standing on a floor on two feet then slowly shift your weight to one foot, it is difficult enough to balance. But when you jump to one foot and try to hold a balanced position before hopping back to the other foot, it is much more difficult. It is this dynamic shifting of balance thousands of times during a tour which is the key to technique.

Balance Exercises

Norway's Olympic skiers practice balance exercises daily. Here are a few exercises to help you with your balance. The first two exercises work on static balance — balance which does not move laterally. The third drill and the skating drills deal with dynamic balance.

One-Leg Balance   *Bent Leg Balance*

Start with one-leg balance exercises. Balance on one foot then the other. Hold the balance on each foot as long as possible. Time yourself on how long you can hold each balanced position. The muscles on the inside and the outside of your hips and thighs both work in this drill. As you start to sway outward, the inside muscles contract. As you start to sway inward, the outside muscles contract.

Balancing on a flexed leg is a bit more difficult. Take your one-foot balance position. Slowly lower your hips until your knee is at about a 60-degree angle. Your hips should be eight to 10 inches lower than in a normal standing position. Move up and down for 15 seconds, or until you have lost your balance. Now do it on the other leg. The same muscles work as in the previous drill, but because you are moving up and down, other muscles come into play and the muscles which hold you balanced must react to different stimuli.

Hopping balance is a more advanced drill. With your weight balanced on one foot, hold for five seconds or until you start to lose your balance then hop to the other foot and hold. Continue hopping from one leg to the other. Learn to hold each new balanced position for five seconds. Start with 6-inch hops. Eventually aim for 24-inch hops.

In this drill the muscles in your legs, which control balance, work as well as the muscles in your hips.If you don't hop far enough outward, the muscles on the outside of your hips must

Rollerblading

149

Rollerblading with poles

work to pull you into the proper position. If you shift too much weight outward, the inner thigh muscles must pull you back or you will fall outward. This drill is critical to teaching your brain just how quickly it must shift the body weight and how far it can shift it.

Dynamic Balance

Roller blades or in-line roller skates as well as roller skis will help you with the dynamic balance needed on the snow. Skiing on in-line skates can be quite easy, especially for skilled skiers. Think about it; you don't have seven feet of ski attached to your feet so the skates are quite easy to turn. The pavement is usually smooth and consistent, and the whole situation is really quite predictable. The skates also hold the road easier than skis hold the snow.

If you are comfortable going left and right while roller skating, start being creative and do some things which will increase your balance on skis. Set up a slalom course. Use rocks, traffic cones or your kids' toys to make a course that you can skate through — just like in the Olympic slalom course. Stagger the "gates," create a course which will challenge your balance — then start skating. Cut left and right, wide turns and sharp turns. Make it fun. It will help you to be a better skater and a better skier.

Another way to develop your skating skills is to play roller hockey. It's a great workout as the spirit of competition motivates you to do some really dumb things. Sprinting for the puck, quick direction changes, and a lot of quick starts and stops are all great for your reactions and coordination. Obviously, you'll want to wear all the protective garb you can get your hands on, as you may well crash occasionally. When you get into it, roller hockey is great for your reactive movements and agility. You'll get in and out of body positions you would never feel going up and down hills. Quite simply, it's a blast, and it will pay great dividends come next season.

Setting gates on a moderately steep road is also a great training aid. It simulates the movements of skiing and can help you to develop an aggressive

Rollerblading with poles

attitude. Set them with lots of turns — short turns, then try to generate speed between the gates. Don't try to improve your technique. Instead, try to acquire that attitude of aggressively going after the next turn rather than waiting for it to come to you. If you can do it on skates, you'll be able to do it on skis.

Play on skates while you increase your sense of balance and equilibrium. It's still important to make some turns, but the emphasis should be toward doing things on skates that allow you to move free from the preoccupation of technique. Learn how to move for balance, not for looks! Also, don't worry about strength or endurance or anaerobic capacity — just make it fun. If you put some chutzpa into the games you play on skates, you'll get stronger, you'll last longer, and you'll have more fun in the process.

Ice skating is another balance activity which you may want to try. For the national ski team in Norway, we bring in the Olympic skating coach to help us with skating technique and balance.

Effective conditioning helps your body to be the best tool that it can be for effective skiing. It also keeps your physiological age reduced. A well-conditioned 60-year-old may have the musculature and heart of a person less than 30. So effective conditioning can make you look and feel better. And certainly it will reduce any unwanted tiredness or soreness on your first tour of the winter!

Epilogue

We have tried to portray the basic principles for Nordic skiing. But remember that each person is a little different. Your skiing will be unique to you. Your technique, just as every other skier from beginner to world champion, will change according to the type of snow, the angle of the slope, speed and level of fatigue. There is no one way to ski — just some basic principles.

And as with any other activity in life, the more you do it, the better you get at it and the more fun it becomes.

So condition yourself, practice your techniques, and ski a lot. And as we say in Norway, "*God tur.*" Have a good tour — through the forests and through your life!

Hot Fun in Cold Weather!

Figure Skating: Sharpen Your Skills
Indiana/World Skating Academy
1-57028-007-X • $14.95

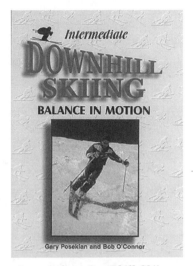

Intermediate Downhill Skiing:
Balance in Motion
Gary Posekian & Bob O'Connor
1-57028-100-9 • $12.95

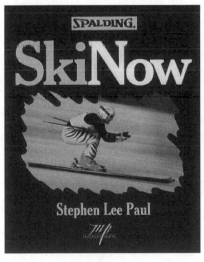

Ski Now
Stephen Lee Paul
1-57028-017-7 • $12.95

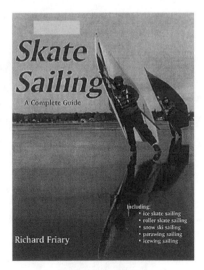

Skate Sailing
Richard Friary
1-57028-098-3 • $19.95

Masters Press has a complete line of winter sports books, and other sports to help coaches and participants alike "master their game."

All of our books are available at better bookstores or by calling Masters Press at 1-800-9-SPORTS. Catalogs available by request.

Ice the Competition!

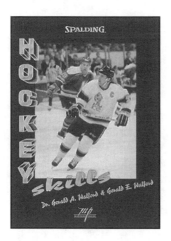

Hockey Skills
Dr. Gerald A. Walford & Gerald E. Walford
0-940279-78-9 • $12.95

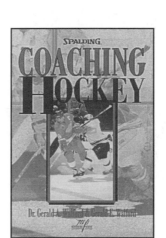

Coaching Hockey
Dr. Gerald A. Walford & Gerald E. Walford
0-940279-79-7 • $12.95

Youth Hockey
Dr. Gerald A. Walford & Gerald E. Walford
0-940279-89-4 • $12.95

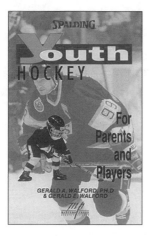

Winning Hockey
Bob Cielo
1-57028-076-2 • $12.95

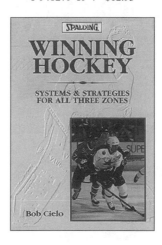

Masters Press has a complete line of hockey books, and other sports to help coaches and participants alike "master their game."

All of our books are available at better bookstores or by calling Masters Press at 1-800-9-SPORTS. Catalogs available by request.